If I Knew Him Then Like I Know Him Now

Wisdom is the principal thing; therefore get wisdom:
and with all thy getting get understanding.
—Proverbs 4:7

Lynette

WESTBOW®
P R E S S
A DIVISION OF THOMAS NELSON
& ZONDERVAN

WestBow Press books may be ordered through booksellers or by contacting:

WestBow Press
A Division of Thomas Nelson
& Zondervan
1663 Liberty Drive
Bloomington, IN 47403
www.westbowpress.com
1 (866) 928-1240

ISBN: 978-1-4908-2271-6 (sc)
ISBN: 978-1-4908-2272-3 (hc)
ISBN: 978-1-4908-2270-9 (e)

Library of Congress Control Number: 2014900694

Printed in the United States of America.

WestBow Press rev. date: 03/21/2014

Contents

Preface

This is a manual to teach others how to recognize and combat the attacks of the adversary. If I had known God back then like I know Him now, I would have avoided many of places I went, people I associated with, and negative positions I found myself in. Almost all of those choices were accompanied by trouble, heartache, and pain. I would not have endured so much grief if I had listened to God, studied His Word, and prayed for His prefect will to be done in my life, while allowing the Holy Spirit to guide and direct me.

Since, I now know God, I can write about some of the real life experiences, hoping to minister to young ladies and to educate women on how to lose the chains that bind them—many of whom are like I once was.

Proverbs 3:5–7 says, "Trust in the LORD with all thine heart; and lean not unto thine own understanding. In all thy ways acknowledge him, and he shall direct thy paths. Be not wise in thine own eyes: fear the LORD, and depart from evil."

This book will discuss a lifestyle, from adolescence to adulthood that is based on trying to live life without a true relationship with God, the only one who can protect us from the agonies of life. Such a lifestyle involves making decisions without divine knowledge, converting one's character to meet everyone else's standards, and losing one's own identity in the process. If I'd had the knowledge back then that I have now, I would have known that the only one who could solidify my worth, my calling, and my life was God.

This biblically based book has statistical data that will show the downward plunge that females have subjected themselves to. As God says in Hosea 4:6, "My people are destroyed from lack of knowledge." Not knowing the devastating results of bad choices will lead women into lives of failure, emptiness, depression, and ultimately destruction. My goal is to expose the disastrous plan that the Devil executes against me, you, your mother, your daughter, your sister, and any other women you may know through the life of Lynette.

This plan is not limited to women. This book will expose and put a halt to the Enemy's hidden agenda for men as it relates to absentee fathers, physical abusers, and user of woman for their own pleasure. It is also meant to be a tool to help men recognize the demonic forces that come against the women in their lives so they can know how to better intercede for them.

God called men to be the head of the house. As women and daughters, we should be able to look to men as our covering for comfort, solace, strength, and protection. But how can men cover and protect us if they are the ones who attack us, leave us to raise kids alone, and fail to train their own children?

The Bible instructs husbands to love their wives as Christ loved the Church and gave Himself for it. What does this mean to a man? Do most men even know how much Christ loved the church? He gave his life for it! This book can challenge men to learn how to become the kings that God has called them to be.

As a daughter, teen, woman, wife, and mother Devil has capitalize on Lynette's mistakes. He tried to hold her in bondage and arrest her development in every stage of life. He attempted to have her physically abused, sexually abused by multiple partners, and raped in two separate attempts. He tried to attack her body, finances, and family to keep her from sharing her story so that others can be free.

One of Satan's tactics is to shut down our lines of communication. He did not want Lynette to share this information, but I could no longer allow his gag order to keep her silent. We are called to share testimonies so that others might be free. Make up your mind today that you will no longer allow the Enemy to hinder or destroy the communication between you and your spouse, your children, and most importantly, God.

I pray that this book prompts a change in the lives of every reader. My prayer is also that God would open each blind eye and every deaf ear to receive the Word of the Lord. In Jesus' name, amen.

How I wish I had known God then like I know Him now.

Foreword

If I knew him then like I know Him Now shares insight that will help readers adjust to the many changes and challenges that life bring you. This shrill wakeup call prompts you to take charge of your life over all the adversities that either has happened is happening or to prevent it from happening. Not only does the author confront areas where subtle passivity or even poor choices may have occurred but also instructs how to avoid or garner up the strength to get out.

If I knew Him then like I know Him Now covers a plethora of societal areas like finances, relationships, and spirituality. It shows how adapting to transitional moments in life is the path to an enriched existence filled with gratification. In If I knew Him then like I know, the author pulls you into the world of a woman and provokes you to reflect rapidly where you are currently and to help you identify and minister to someone who is going through similar situations.

This book will incite rage to the camp of the enemy because it testifies of his plans to kill your dream, steal your prosperity and to destroy your relationships. She also enthralls you with Lynette's triumphs over these "could be" and "would be" devastating and life threatening situation. If I knew Him Then like I Know Him now will thrust you into interrogating your life, your relationships, how you allocate your finances, and it give insight on ungodly predators that have entered your spirit! This is truly a must read.

Apostle T. Anthony Williams

Acknowledgments

To my mom: I thank you for showing me how to be a true woman of courage, honor, support, and protection for my family. Without your strength, I would not be here today. You have taught me how to be a strong woman and that my fight does not have to be with my fist. Watching you has taught me how to be a survivor and never to give up, no matter how tough things get. Thanks, Mom, for being my friend and encourager. I love you dearly.

To my children: Because of you guys, I became a better mother and person. I learned how to sacrifice and put other needs above my own. I thank you, and I love each one of you. To my siblings: Each of you has contributed something different into my life, all of which taught me how to be a better listener and caring sister.

To my best friends: We have been through many trials and tribulations, but we've seen each other through. You guys helped me to keep it real, and I thank you for your sisterhood. To all my exes: I thank you. Your deceptions, manipulations, and abusiveness forced me to be the strong, determined black woman I am today.

I would like to give special thanks to my husband and best friend, the apostle and priest of my home: You are a godsend. You have been my spiritual backbone. Without your support, words of encouragement, prayers, and love, I would not have completed this project. I love you, honey, and I thank God for your loving heart and your submissive spirit. May God bless you always!

Most importantly, I thank my heavenly Father for impregnating me with this book and helping me birth it. Father, You have allowed me to deliver this book, thus freeing me from the trouble, heartache, and pain that life brings. Thank you, Lord, for all the love, grace, and favor that you bestow upon my life. It has taken me places that my character couldn't.

CHAPTER 1

Genesis: The Beginning of Time

In the beginning was the Word, and the Word was with God, and
the Word was God. The same was in the beginning with God. All
things were made by him; and without him was not any thing made
that was made. In him was life; and the life was the light of men.
—John 1:1–4

It was the summer of 1976. Lynette was thirteen years old and had applied
for her very first job. Although she knew she had to be at least fifteen
years old to work, she thought she was the exception to the rule, and she
decided to fill out the application anyway. She met with a man by the
name of Troy Harris, who was the director of the youth program and the
hiring manager. As he critiqued her paperwork, he explained to her what
she already knew. "You are not old enough to work," he told her.

Lynette was a very persistent young girl, who could not take no for an
answer. She talked and talked until she was able to persuade Troy that
she would be the best worker he would ever hire. Troy was so impressed
that he altered Lynette's paperwork, giving her the opportunity to prove
herself.

Wow, I am so excited! she thought. *This is going to be the best summer ever. I
have my first job, and I'm going to have my own money and be able to buy my
own clothes. This is the best day ever.*

Lynette worked as a camp counselor for a local youth center. There were many neighborhood youths who worked there as well. Some she knew, and others she had not seen before. Each morning they met in the same room to get their assignments, and every morning the same young man sat across the room from Lynette, staring at her. He was tall and thin and had a lot of hair.

One morning Lynette's best friend Rita told her, "Girl, he is staring at you again." Lynette was not used to this type of attention, and she was an immature and very angry young girl. The stares of this young man made her very uncomfortable. She knew nothing about boys or having boyfriends, so she did what every young angry, unconcern, thirteen-year-old would do. She yelled, "What are you looking at?"

Lynette's attitude was bad. Her dad had left home when she was ten years old, and her mom was dealing with her own problems that she did not recognize Lynette's anger and pain. Lynette was surrounded by people who were much older than she was, and she was too immature to understand what was happening. She had never encountered dating, flirting, or being around older, more experienced boys. Although Lynette had thought this job was a good thing for her, she had placed herself in a position where she was going to be forced to encounter some things she was not ready for.

Note to parents: Please make sure you are not exposing your children to too much too soon. Doing so places them in positions they are not ready to handle and causes them to advance ahead of their years.

Lynette was very naive; and as long as things were hidden from her, she had no interest in them. The unfortunate part of this was that once she was exposed to things, curiosity took over. Weeks into the job, she realized that boys were noticing her. Lynette had just graduated from eighth grade, so she was starting to enter a whole new world. Most of these young men were already in high school, making her feel inadequate to even engage in small talk without feeling uncomfortable.

This was the start of the rumbling volcano that began to express the essence of her identity. Each passing day, she noticed places that had been straight and flat before were beginning to fill out with bumps and curves. A metamorphosis was taking place in her body that she had not known existed. Her femininity started spewing out like water. She had a new walk, a new talk, and a new attitude. Lynette's skirts got shorter, pants tighter, eyes more flirtatious, and her smile much brighter as she transformed into young adulthood.

Was she ready for all the attention her new look was going to give her? Had she matured enough to handle the looks, whistles, and stares? Only weeks earlier, she had yelled at a young man just for looking at her. What about the more advanced issues, like dating, sex, and pregnancy that she might stumble upon with her new look, new attitude, and new mind-set? She didn't realize that she was not mentally, physically, or emotionally ready to engage in a relationship that could open the window to sex, teen violence, pregnancy, sexually transmitted diseases (STD), and ungodly soul ties.

For weeks Lynette and other young ladies sashayed around, competing for the young men's attention. She quickly transformed from an innocent young girl into a power-seeking young seductress. She too wanted the boys to notice her, and she would have done almost anything to accomplish this goal. She learned the strategy for getting boys to notice her without doing anything or saying a word. She learned how to leave an impression by just entering and exiting a room.

Lynette did not have a boyfriend and was not interested in getting one. She just liked the control she had to move the crowd. Was she becoming a tease? Was she dressing provocatively to win the attention of the guys? Yes, and worse than that, Lynette was becoming the kind of person she had once despised—the kind of girl who used her body to get what she wanted from a man, the type who would flirt with a man just to control and seduce him. Where did this ungodly spirit come from, and how did it gain entry into her life? She must have ushered it in without even realizing it.

Note to men: this type of behavior is known to lure you into a lustful and vulnerable state, only to be sifted like wheat by the Enemy.

"For why should you, her son, be enraptured by an immoral woman, and be embraced in the arms of a seductress?" (Proverbs 5:20). The entire book of Proverbs was written to instruct men on how to be wise to the traps and schemes of seductive women. Solomon, the author of Proverbs, warned men not to be drawn and carried away by a beautiful woman. He described the process as being parallel to an animal being led to the slaughter house (Proverbs 7:22). This is also a call to women not to be led astray by men who know how to seduce them and lure them away from the things of God.

In the book of Judges, the sixteenth chapter, a young man by the name of Samson was mighty in strength, but he failed in weakness when he was enticed by a beautiful woman named Delilah. The Bible illustrates how strong Samson was—so strong that he killed a lion with his bare hands, gathered and tied three hundred foxes together by their tails, and killed thousands of Philistine soldiers with the jawbone of a donkey. Since he was undefeated, the Philistines were determined to find the key to his strength, and they bribed Delilah to help them. Using seduction, she teased him until he revealed to her the secret to his amazing strength. According to the biblical account, Samson's strength was in his hair, and he had been commanded never to cut it. Once he felt asleep, Delilah called in the Philistines to cut his hair, and he was turned over to his enemies.

There is no description of Delilah's beauty, but I can imagine her being the "Beyonce" or "Halle Berry" type of woman who can take a man's breath away, or a woman who knows how to devour a man whole and render him helpless. The Bible never mentions whether Samson and Delilah had an affair, but he allowed himself to enter into an ungodly relationship with her.

The spirit of Delilah is wrapped in a beautiful package, and it comes with a manipulative and destructive spirit. It has affected many men, women, teens, husbands, wives, presidents, churches, and even you. The only mission of this type of spirit is to bring you down and leave you powerless. It destroys your soul and separates you from the protection of God.

Your soul carries your intellect, your emotions, and your will. Thus, you should guard it from people who set out to control and dominate you with smooth talk, body talk, eye talk, or money talk. You can be seduced and lose all you have, because the "game" is to steal your heart, destroy your mind, and kill your soul.

Relationships are not always sexual, but a bond can develop between any two people who open themselves up to one another. The strength of the bond between you and another person depends on how deeply you are involved with them. The people you allow to come into your life can influence and shape you, and they can hinder your walk with Christ. In ungodly relationships, you will find yourself doing things you would never have thought of on your own.

You need to check the motives of the person you are with. If Lynette had known during her teen years the things she know now, she would not have found herself in relationships with men who were controlling, manipulative, abusive, self-centered, and unhealthy.

This chapter is called "Genesis," because it defines the sequences that framed Lynette's life. It is the beginning of becoming something. One of the areas of study in psychology is mental function and behavior. In the eight stages of development, according to psychologist Erik Erikson, one must complete the first stage in order to successfully move to the next. Aaron Beck's *Cognitive Therapy* suggests that if we can tap into the way a person thinks (cognition), we can change the negative and destructive thinking (behavior).

Lynette's behavior did not truly begin at fourteen (adolescence) but at ten, the year her father walked out on her. At this stage, she had not yet developed a sense of the cause-and-effect of her actions, and she did not have self-confidence or moral values. She had no outside interests, and obtaining a job at such a young age caused her to skip right past her teen years, from childhood into adulthood.

The teen years can encompass some rough times, because that's when young people begin to make their own decisions as they move into adulthood. If a stage is missed, it can cause role confusion and identity crisis. If a person doesn't have a solid foundation, they will crack under pressure like thin ice.

At fourteen, Lynette began to date, which she was not ready to do. This also was the time when her environment began to shape her into the kind of person she was becoming. She crumbled under peer pressure, which caused her to be in situations she had no real understanding of.

Lynette's life is like the folktale, "Little Red Riding Hood." We all know the story about a young, virtuous girl skipping through the woods to her grandma's house. There was a song that depicted one of many interpretations of this story. The song was entitled "Olivia" and was sung by one of Lynette's favorite groups.

Olivia got distracted on her way
To grandmother's house
A wolf in nice clothin' came
Blew her mind and changed her ways

In this song, and in the lives of today's youth, young people encounter various wolves, which come in the form of good intentions and good moral character but are nothing more than physical abusers, users for pleasure, or mind manipulators. In the Bible, God warns us about such wolves. "Behold, I send you forth as sheep in the midst of wolves: be ye therefore wise as serpents, and harmless as doves. But beware of men: for they will deliver you up to the councils, and they will scourge you in their synagogues" (Matthew 10:16–17).

Wolves are deceitful in all their ways and come dressed in many different disguises. They come with apparent gentleness, love, care, patience, and kindness. Most teens are so trusting and naive that they unknowingly give these wolves vital information that can hinder or abort their destiny. That is why they need to be careful of what they put on My Space, Twitter, and Facebook. There is no reason why people need to update their whereabouts and give the world too much information, because no one is that important. What may start out as a joke or a way of conversing with Internet pals allows pedophiles and molesters to use this information to gain illegal access to people.

We must equip our young people to protect themselves from the Enemy's hidden agenda. Just like the story of Little Red Riding Hood, many of today's youths go skipping from childhood to adulthood through the woods of life, not knowing what lies ahead. Although this road of transformation appears easy, there are many wolves lurking, plotting, and scheming, waiting for their easy young prey.

Teens cannot afford to be blinded by the ever present danger of wolves that are hiding in the bushes, waiting to steal their basket of goodies. It doesn't manner if you are old school or a new school; your basket of goodies represent purity and it is not meant to be shared among the crowd. If you are not married, you are to keep yourself pure until that time, because your innocence is what the wolves are really after.

"In the beginning God created the heaven and the earth. And the earth was without form, and void; and darkness was upon the face of the deep. And the Spirit of God moved upon the face of the waters. And God said, Let there be light: and there was light. And God saw the light, that it was good: and God divided the light from the darkness" (Genesis 1:14).

When God called Lynette out of her darkness and into His marvelous light, she too was without form and void. She was empty and had no self-esteem or self-worth. That state left her open to physical, emotional, and psychological abuse. She needed to be delivered and set free so that she could help others. She came up with every excuse as to why she was not qualified or ready to tell her story, but when God showed her the many plagues that were killing His people, she knew her testimony was not for her but to help others. She wanted to help God's people get delivered from the slavery of the Pharaohs, and the demonic forces that rule and control their lives.

I am sure that if we could all go back and talk to our younger selves, we would. Since Lynette cannot go back and talk to her younger self, she decided to come forth and share with you, so that you don't have to *wish* you knew–you shall know. God uses common folk like Lynette to do His will. He used Moses to free the children of Israel. He used Noah to restore humanity. He used Joseph to lead His people, and He is still using people today. God asked, "Lynette, are you willing to share your story so that purity can be restored to children?" She answered and said, "Lord, send me. I will go."

Lynette had to be willing to open herself up to be humiliated so that she might help others. Coitus has taken over our children's lives, through dancing, music, airwaves, and computers. Intimacy is beautiful, because God designed it, and it is a gift to be shared under the covenant of marriage. Such intimacy outside of marriage is sin. In July 2003 the Lord healed Lynette from all her soul ties and set her free from all her past sins, hurts, and errors so that she could be strong enough to share her story with you.

You can start your healing process if you open your heart and say yes to God's will and ways. Lynette will share her past with you, so that you can see where you are in your present and move toward your future. Here's her story.

"When they teach someone what they have learned, they learn twice; once when they receive and again when they give. Receiving begins the learning process; teaching someone else completes it" (Stephen Covey).

CHAPTER 2

Flamin' Hot: Sin and Shame

"For surely I know the plans I have for you," says the LORD, "plans to prosper you and not to harm you, plans to give you hope and a future."
—Jeremiah 29:11 NIV

Anthony was his name, and he worked with Lynette at the local youth center. In fact, he was the same young man Lynette had previously yelled at just for looking at her. He carried a huge radio everywhere, blasting it down the street. He was in charge of the summer sports tournaments at the youth center. Anthony appeared to be sweet, and because he was a star on the court, young ladies were always around him. Lynette knew she was not experienced enough to know a "good man" if she saw one, but these ladies seemed so desperate to get this man's attention and that drew Lynette in for a closer look.

The job seemed more like a vacation, because they were getting paid to have fun. Anthony and Lynette worked on the same assignment, which meant they were together often. They coached and played volleyball, softball, and basketball. She was not as good as some of the other young ladies, because most of them were on the basketball team at one of the local high schools. Even though she did not know how to play basketball, it apparently did not matter to Anthony, because he always chose her to play on his team.

Lynette started feeling comfortable enough having Anthony around that she allowed him to come over to her house after work and even on weekends. The first time he asked her out on a real date, she told him that she would only go if he took her girlfriend Rita as well. It was not normal for a boy to be forced to entertain two people just because he liked one of them. Lynette wanted Rita to accompany her on this date, because she had never fully developed during the prior stage of her life, and she did not understand the whole dating thing.

Lynette believed that Anthony was already sexually active, and he could have felt that he was wasting his time with her. In fact, there was a young lady named Sandy who lived on Anthony's block, and Lynette recalled her coming on the job and making waves because Anthony was supposed to be her man and she'd heard that he was cheating on her. Sandy and Lynette attended the same school, and rumor had it that Sandy had a baby and that Anthony was supposed to be the father. Was this a red flag, a warning to Lynette that if Anthony was denying his child, she could find herself in that situation one day? Was this a sign that Lynette should have stayed away? If Sandy and Anthony were in a prior relationship and Sandy had a baby, surely they were connected.

The summer job had ended, and it was time for Lynette to get ready for school. She started high school and began to enjoy and appreciate young men. She had male friends from school that she was able to hang out with—without the pressure of giving of herself. Tryouts for the pom-pom squad were in two weeks. With hard work and long practices, she made the team. She met many people because of her position on the squad.

Tim was one of her male friends and he was on the basketball team. As they began to hang out, she noticed that Tim wanted more. He began pressuring her to get involved in something she wasn't ready for. He made statements like, "If you like me and want to remain friends, show me." Because Lynette was not experienced with dating, she asked, "What do you mean?" He answered, "You can show how much you care about me by connecting with me intimately."

She was gripped with fear and remembered eavesdropping on her brother's conversations with his friends about the girls in the neighborhood, including the jokes and names they called them. Lynette visualized how her dad and other men in her circle of influence treated women, and she vowed never to allow men to disrespect her. She told Tim, "I am not ready for that, and if it's your only reason for hanging out with me, then you are wasting your time."

Despite Lynette's expressed feelings, Tim became more demanding, and she decided to stop hanging out with him. She was determined not to let Tim or anyone else persist in behavior that forced her into a relationship—regardless of what her peers thought. Once the guys heard about her "so-call break up" and that she was spending time with Craig (who happened to be on the football team), Lynette was accused of being a "seasonal girl." The term "seasonal girl" meant that the girl would only hang out with or date guys who played ball during that particular season.

Teens can be so cruel. What would make them say such lies about her? Tim had started spreading rumors about her in an attempt to destroy her reputation for not sleeping with him.

Lynette had to take a look at herself to see why these things were being said. She was not sexually active, and the lies about her were hurtful; they were an attack on her character. Was she putting herself out there in such a way that people labeled her as being easy and loose? Was it in the way she walked, her conversations, or the clothes she wore? Was Lynette sending mixed messages that suggested she was promiscuous? Was she carrying a certain spirit that she was not aware of? Should she be concerned with what others thoughts about her, or should she just ignored them and move on?

In the middle of the school year, Troy Harris contacted Lynette and offered her a part-time position at the youth center. On her first day on the job, she ran into—that's right—Anthony. The last time they had seen each other was the night of their so-called date. They joked about that night, and as she explained to Anthony all the negative names she had been called at school, they decided to give this dating thing a try. Lynette was surprised to find out that Anthony and Tim were next-door neighbors. This may have made her looked like a "seasonal girl" again, but she knew the truth about herself, so she ignored the lies.

Note to adults: If you are going to give "the sex talk," please give examples, testimonies, and statistics. That spiel of "don't do *it* because I said so," does not work. It only intensifies the urge to pursue and experience. By the way, just because you decided to ignore the issue will not make it go away.

Lynette's supervisor Troy noticed how close Anthony and Lynette was getting, so he decided to educate them about contraceptives and sexually transmitted diseases (STDs). He felt that he could not stop them from engaging, but he felt obligated to tell them about protection. *Here we go again*, Lynette thought. Here she was, talking to her male supervisor about relationships. It was the second time she had been confronted with this topic. Sure, her mother had told her not to do *it*, but things were different when you are face-to-face with the challenge.

Will you be able to stand for righteousness when you are faced with a test or trial? Can you say no when you are faced with your own temptations? How much of what you have been taught can you apply to decision-making? Are you equipped to handle those challenges life brings your way?

If I could have shared what I know now with little Lynette back then, she would have been shown the trap that was set before her. This area of her life was becoming a struggle for her because of the heat and pressure within. Satan knew that once this sin had been introduced to Lynette, she would become inquisitive.

She started seeing and hearing more and more about the subject. It was everywhere. Tim had exposed her to the idea of having sex, and Troy had introduced a new thought about the different contraceptives available to protect her from pregnancy. Now it had become something she had to research. She found out that everyone was "doing it," from her best friend to every girl on the cheerleading and pom-pom squads.

To fit in, she had to pretend that she was partaking in the sinful pleasure, when in fact it was something she knew nothing about. Lynette made up fake stories about times and places, the joy and pain—repeating things she heard other girls speak about. However, Lynette lost her virginity at the age of sixteen. At that time, she engaged in sex only because everyone else was doing it. She felt left out, pressured, and afraid—all because of this one thing.

Note to parents: Your daughter or son may go to prom as a virgin, but he or she may not come home as one. For most high school seniors, the idea of a great prom includes alcohol and sex. Please make sure you talk with your child so that his or her first experience won't be in the backseat of someone's car and get posted on the Internet.

Anthony was two grades ahead of Lynette. He was approaching his senior year and asked Lynette to accompany him to the prom. This was also the night that she tried sex for the very first time, the night she lost her virginity. Soon afterward, Anthony and Lynette starting making out all the time. She felt the need to engage him so he wouldn't have a desire to be with anyone else. This was going to work, right? The two of them were intimate so often that she became addicted. He was like a drug dealer; he'd talked her into trying sex with him, so he was the one she would come back to for it. It became more than something she did every now and then. It became an ungodly habit.

Everything she knew, heard, and was taught about love was not true, and it had a lasting effect on her life. This act of sin had a grip so tight on her that she did not even recognize that she had become captivated. If I'd known how to reach the younger Lynette, I would have let her know that once you have allowed yourself to engage in this sin, you have opened yourself up for the Devil to assault you mentally, physically, emotionally, and spiritually. This act is more than just a physical attraction. Rather, your body and the body of your partner become one. You have now entered into a certain kind of bondage, and it has turned into an ungodly soul tie.

As Christians we are not supposed to allow sin to cripple us. If I had known God then, I would have told Lynette and others like her that just having a religion and being baptized was not good enough. They needed a relationship with God and more associations with godly people. Although Lynette had given her life over to God at the age of twelve, her actions did not reflect godly behavior. Somewhere along the way, she had missed the lesson that the church taught about how to put on the full armor of God in order to combat the attacks of the Enemy.

Whom could she confide in? Everyone she knew was in the same boat she was. What had happened to all her godly friends and influences? Has she surrounded herself with people who did not care about their salvation either? How had Lynette gotten so entangled in all these ungodly relationships?

"What? know ye not that he which is joined to an harlot is one body? For two, saith he, shall be one flesh" (1 Corinthians 6:16). Ungodly soul ties are when two souls are knitted or cleaved together, forming bondage and a type of enslavement. When you become involved, you are taking fragments of the soul and leaving it with your partner. For this reason, many cannot commit to marriage or a monogamous relationship, because their emotions are drawn to past partners. This is true of anyone who is a victim of rape or molestation as well. For more on soul ties, visit this websites: www.b4prayer.org/index11.html.

Note to parents: Monitor the people you allow your kids to hang out with. You also need to check out the music they listen to, the movies they watch, and the videos they play. All these things carry some type of spirit that will begin to show up your child's behavior in some noticeable way. "Can a man take fire in his bosom, and his clothes not be burned?" (Proverbs 6:27).

This ungodly act of sin affected Lynette's reproductive system. No, there was nothing wrong. It just started to produce. In her second year of high school, Lynette became pregnant. Silly girl, thinking that being sexually active had helped her develop from a frail young girl into an attractive young woman. Her behavior should have told someone that she was not ready for what had been designed for the marital unit. The fact that she was no longer clumsy and walked with a more confident and assured strut were telltale signs that she had entered into a world that she was not ready for.

Anthony confronted Lynette about being pregnant. He only knew about it because his mom had told him she was. Anthony's mom knew that Anthony and Lynette were making out in her home, and she definitely knew that Lynette was pregnant. As women, we should know our body. The symptoms of menstruation are similar to those of pregnancy. They affect three areas: physical, emotional, and behavioral. Some physical effects are headache, bloating, nausea, and vomiting. In one survey, 68 percent of women experienced breast symptoms associated with menstruation. Emotionally, women can become depressed, anxious, irritable, and hostile. Their behavioral symptoms can include mood swings, withdrawal, and fatigue.

Facts: Fifty percent of teens get pregnant during the first four months of unprotected sex. Seventy-five percent become pregnant in eight months, and ninety percent are pregnant within a year.

Lynette, was ashamed of what she had done and the people she had let down. She wore her clothes bigger so that others would not know that she was pregnant. I am sure the Devil was laughing and telling God about what Lynette had done, even as she was looking crazy and feeling sorry and embarrassed. The trouble has just begun, because now she had to find a way to inform her mom.

Lynette's mom Margie was in her room, hanging up some clothes, when Lynette came and sat on her bed. "Mom," she said, "I need to talk to you." Anyone who knows Lynette's mom knows that one did not enter her bedroom—and most definitely did not sit on her bed.

Lynette joked around about what she was going to give her mom for Christmas, and out of the blue she asked, "What if I told you that you were going to be a grandmother?" Her mom never even stopped to look at her. She gently said, "You must have lost your mind. You cannot afford to have a baby." Before Lynette could think, she blurted out, "You don't know what I could afford." She knew right then that her mother was trying to be patient with her. If she had known what was best for her, she would have left right then, unassisted.

Note to parents: You need to monitor the behavior of your children. If your child has a friend of the opposite sex, and they are spending countless hours alone, they could be sexually active. This can now be true with friends of the same gender.

Your child is probably active if he or she would rather suffer the consequences of your punishments than miss seeing this friend. If your child is willing to lie and sneak to see this friend, your kid is most likely active. In order to detect this, it requires spending time with them.

I can imagine that if you are a parent reading this, you are saying or thinking, "I have enough to do without spending time questioning my child's every move." If you are a teen mom, you are probably saying, "Yeah, if my mom would have spent more time with me, caring and asking questions, I would not have gotten myself in this situation."

Fathers are, by no means, exempt from their roles and responsibilities. If the truth were told, they are more at fault for not being around to teach their daughters how to honor and respect themselves. Little girls search for love from other men because of the insecurities created by their own fathers' absence. Daughters suffer from lack of love, support, teaching, and parenting from their fathers. A father should be there when Ray Ray comes knocking on the door to pick up his princess. A father should warn those guys that he is not going to allow them to mess up his daughter's life.

Lynette transferred to another school that was suited for pregnant teens. She heard about it from a young lady who happened to come from the same high school she attended. As they began to chat and share stories about the young men they dated, this young lady started asking more probing questions about Anthony. She later informed Lynette that he sounded like the same guy her sister was dating. She told Lynette that Anthony was spending countless hours with her sister.

After he was confronted with his deceitfulness, Anthony explained that he was trying to teach Lynette a lesson. He wanted her to see what a good catch he was and that any woman would be glad to be with him. Since Lynette was young, immature, and pregnant, this made sense to her, so she decided to forgive him and move on.

If only I could have warned young Lynette then, I would have told her that the Devil had a trap, a scheme, and a plan for her demise. I would have reminded her of the day when that young lady Sandy had confronted Anthony earlier about his cheating ways. It was a warning sign that she should never have ignored, but because she had low self-esteem and no self-worth, it was easy for her to be lured into a path of unrighteous and ungodly acts.

If only I could have reached that young lady then, I would have told her that setting goals for herself would have prevented her from being easy prey for her own idle mind. Lack of will and knowledge, accompanied by immaturity, had her bound at the young age of seventeen. Setting goals would have helped her become what God had designed her to be. Knowing where she wanted to be and concentrating on the task of getting there would have placed her in a better position, and she would have known that Anthony and many like him were a distraction that would try to keep her from her destiny.

If you are in a position where things seem hopeless, take some time right now to set some goals. Knowing what you want in life and finding your niche will help you set your sights on achievements and will challenge you to want more. If you are a teen reading this, do not make the same mistake Lynette made. You can know now, rather than later, the consequences of making the wrong choice. You do not have to perish for lack of knowledge. If Lynette had had something or someone to teach her and share with her how to tap into her gifts and talents, she would not have waited until she was an adult to go back to school. She always had desires but no drive. It took her twenty years to realize her purpose in life.

I put a charge on all parents, teachers—and even you—to speak a blessing into the lives of your sons, daughters, nieces, nephews, students, and neighbors' children. We have a duty to our children to recognize their gifts, talents, and callings and to speak life into them. We need to encourage our young, intelligent sons and daughters, telling them that they too can succeed in life.

Oprah Winfrey and Donald Trump succeeded, not only because of their desires but because someone believed in them and pushed them to achieve their goals. If only Lynette had known then that "where there is no vision, the people perish" (Proverbs 29:18). She was on a path that was leading to failure, because she failed to set goals.

When teens become parents, they are usually still living at home, are still in high school, and have no clue how to provide for a child. There she was, a seventeen-year-old mother with no job. Lynette had no plans for college and no wedding in sight. She walked around as though all was well. She did not understand the damage she had done to her body and soul. This is not to say that she could not have picked up the pieces of her life and move on. The question was, *how?*

How could she go on her merry way and start fresh? Where could she begin? Would she have time to be a mother and a student? Should she forget school and find a job? Who would watch her baby? How would she get to work? Who, what, where, when, why, how? All these questions filled her head, but she had no clue as to what to do.

Fact: teen moms are less likely to finish high school, will probably have to rely on public assistance, and are generally not employable and less likely to get married.

Lynette's mom provided things for her daughter. Her sisters watched the baby so that Lynette could get some sleep, do homework, and work her part-time job. Everything was working out fine, right? Wrong. The baby's crying tantrums at 1:00 a.m. were not pretty. She cried for what seemed like hours, even when she was not wet or hungry. So why was she crying? Lynette was not the most well-liked person in her household, because this became a nightly routine for her, the baby, and the entire family.

Fact: According to the National Center for Health Statistics, roughly one half of all pregnancies in the United States are unintended. In 2006–2010 one in nine sexually experienced women aged fifteen to forty-four had used emergency contraception at least once. Over-use of emergency contraception was most common among women aged twenty to twenty-four who had never married, Hispanic or non-Hispanic white women, and those who attended college. Most women who had used emergency contraception had done so once or twice. For more information on this or related topics, visit www.cdc.gov/nchs/data/databriefs/db112.pdf.

Marriage was designed to be the foundation within which children are born. According to the Word of God, Genesis 1:28 says that God told Adam and Eve to be fruitful and multiply and replenish the earth. This decree was only given to couples in marriage. The Bible does not talk about birth control but says that children are a gift from God. "Lo, children are an heritage of the LORD: and the fruit of the womb is his reward. As arrows are in the hand of a mighty man; so are children of the youth. Happy is the man that hath his quiver full of them: they shall not be ashamed, but they shall speak with the enemies in the gate" (Psalm 127:3–5). Children are considered one's strength (Genesis 49:3), because it takes strength to conceive. Childbearing is taken so lightly that abortion and other methods to stop conception have become million-dollar market each year.

Three years later came "Plan B." No, it was not the morning-after pill; it was a second pregnancy! Anthony had cheated again, and this time Lynette had contracted an STD. She was at home with her mom and sister, when there was a knock at the door. Upon answering the knock, Lynette discovered two fully dressed nuns. Being raised as a Baptist, Lynette knew a little about Jehovah's Witnesses, but she was certain they did not make house calls in habits. What were these nuns doing at her front door? she wondered. Lynette's mother invited them in, and they asked to speak with Lynette. Then they informed her, she had to come to the clinic to be treated for Chlamydia. What?

Fact: abstinence is the safest and most convenient method to prevent unwanted pregnancies and too protect you from STDs.

Tears filled Lynette's eyes with the horror and shock of the news. "What is that?" she asked. "It's an STD," one responded. Those two old ladies gave Lynette a piercing look and informed her that if she did not get treated within twenty-four hours she could be arrested for endangering her unborn child.

Fact: Regardless of whether or not you are in a monogamous relationship, STDs do not discriminate against social status, educational level, age, race, or religion. If you are actively engaging in sex, you are at risk. There are thousands of newly reported cases of varies STDs each year, and if they go untreated, they can cause serious harm to yourself and your partner. If you are pregnant, it is even more serious and life-threatening for you and your unborn child.

STDs can pass to the baby before, during, and after birth. They can cause the baby to have pneumonia, blindness, or brain damage—and at worst, stillbirth. For more information about sexually transmitted diseases, visit the website for the Center for Disease Control and Prevention at www.cdc.gov/std/STDFact-STDs&Pregnancy.htm.

Lynette called her doctor, and he set up an appointment for her the next day at the free clinic. As she walked in, she was handed a pile of paperwork to complete, but before she could even finish reading the first form, she was immediately called up. She stood up and was directed to enter the back of another room, where there sat ten or more women. Without any privacy, she was handed about twelve "horse" pills. As she choked to swallow the pills, she could hear the women whispering.

Some thought Lynette had neglected prenatal care and was being forced to take the pills, while others stated that she must be a pregnant drug abuser. She turned to scan the room and noticed all the ladies looking at her. She yelled, "What are you looking at?" Was there no end to the embarrassment? A feeling of shame covered her like a blanket. If only Lynette had known then that sin exposes you to the world. It tells others that you are involved in something that not only humiliates you but your entire family.

Have you ever noticed that when people are "caught," they almost always hide their faces from the cameras? Where were the embarrassment and guilt when they were out committing the crime? People walk around thinking no one will ever find out what they do in the dark, but like the old saying goes, "What's done in the dark will eventually come to the light."

Lynette's shame was so deep that it was toxic. There she sat, pregnant with a second baby and unmarried—and, on top of all that, she had an STD. Toxic shame occurs when you are exposed—either unexpectedly or before you are ready to be exposed—making you helpless and powerless, which is what sin does to the soul. For more on toxic shame, visit www. soulselfhelp.on.ca/tshame.html.

She felt the scrutinizing eyes of the other women in the clinic, because that scrutiny had internalized itself, and she was angry and melancholic. It was easy to admit to others that she was afraid or at fault, but her embarrassment and shame kept her isolated and empty. She felt like a complete failure. After taking the antibiotics, an older lady consoled her, explaining that she too was there because her mate had given her the same STD. In fact, each woman in the room had an STD. These women were either on drugs or were low-income women who could not afford prenatal care. Some were even prostitutes.

STDs have now escalated from syphilis, chlamydia, and gonorrhea to HIV and AIDS, and people are doing more than just taking a handful of pills: they are dying at an alarming rate. The worst part about this is that not everyone will have the resources or money to receive the drugs to combat this deadly disease.

Facts: Worldwide, HIV/AIDS has claimed the lives of over twenty-five million people. Since 2008, 33.3 million women and 15.7 million children are living with HIV/AIDS. According to the Center for Disease Control, women account for one in four people living with HIV in the United States. African American women and Latinas are disproportionately affected at all stages of HIV infection. For more information about pregnant women and HIV, visit www.cdc.gov/hiv/risk/gender/pregnantwomen/facts/index.html.

As Lynette left that place, her mind was racing and blood boiling. She could not wait to see this infectious cheater. When she made it home, her mom tried to comfort her, but the only thing she could think about was the shame her sin had caused. Whatever sin you are caught in, it will surely bring you shame.

Two kids later, Lynette finally woke up and realized that this relationship was not working for her. What must she do to ensure that she could make it without the support she was getting from Anthony? In her early twenties with two kids, what could she do? What *must* she do? She needed to be able to support her kids, and she needed to start somewhere. *I know what I can do,* she thought. *I can get a better paying job.* And that was exactly what Lynette did. She went to as many companies as she could, filling out applications. She was finally called for an interview.

Fact: You have to be exceptionally talented to defy the odds against making a decent salary without college.

Anthony wanted to make things right, now that he saw that Lynette had some determination and strength to move on. Now he saw the worth of a "sista and all-in love."

"What's love got to do with it?" she yelled. Anthony did not love her; he only loved the thing she supplied: her body. "Flamin' hot" describes what the body goes through as the thought of sinful pleasure consumes you. It is like a volcanic eruption, and it illustrates how the body is moved by some force of energy that goes to the mind. The thought of this energy goes deep into the heart and as the thought increases, your temperature rises and the body starts to "flame."

This metamorphosis portrays the many changes that youth experience in their bodies. Desire is stirred, and the sex drive is activated. It is a consuming fire, and if you are not operating within the will of God, the fires of your sinful nature will definitely burn within, and you will begin to operate in the lust of the flesh. Make up your mind today that you will never again allow your flesh or any other sin to consume you. Be set free and take control of yourself. Never again allow the spirit of lust, adultery, and fornication to destroy your life—in the name of Jesus, amen.

"I say then: Walk in the Spirit, and you shall not fulfill the lust of the flesh. For the flesh lusts against the Spirit, and the Spirit against the flesh; and these are contrary to one another, so that you do not do the things that you wish" (Galatians 5:16–17 NKJV).

CHAPTER 3

Revenge: Sweet or Sour

Dearly beloved, avenge not yourselves, but rather give place unto
wrath: for it is written, Vengeance is mine; I will repay, saith the Lord.
—Romans 12:19

Lynette arrived at her interview early, and the receptionist ushered
her in the waiting room of a small office. Moments later she said, "Ms.
Lynette, Mr. Cary is ready to see you now." Lynette had studied the
typical interview questions, and she was ready, her heart pumping with
excitement. She entered another room where she met the man who was
going to interview her. They sat there quietly for what seemed to be
forever. Lynette decided to take control of the conversation but was
stopped cold.

He continued to look her up and down, as if he was undressing her with
his eyes. Just as she started to speak again, he began telling her that he
wanted to offer her a position different from the one she had applied for.
As he explained the duties of the new job, the thing that drew her was
the pay. He was offering more money to do less work. What a deal! She
was hired on the spot and was to start the very next day. The not-so-good
thing about his whole process was that she left the interview feeling like
she had just been assaulted.

She started her new job as an elevator operator. What a cushy job! All
she had to do was sit, wait, and go. She came into contact with many of

the patrons, and as a result, she was approached by many men who tried to take her out on a date. They were from all ethnicities and social and marital status.

Note to women: Don't date married men. When a man has the audacity to approach you, and the ring is an indication that he is married, send him on his "marry" way. Together, we can stop adultery by putting ourselves in the wife's shoes. This also goes for men who find joy in taking another man's wife as their own.

Lynette may have been many things, but she did not like "M&M's" (married men) approaching her, and when they did, she would give them a few choice words. She was so loud that the patrons began waiting for the doors to open to see who she was going-off on this time. Her manager heard about her outbursts and warned her to find a better way to get her point across. He also told her that she needed to get over it, because her looks were the only reason he had hired her.

Note to women: How long will we allow ourselves to be sexually exploited? We are plastered all over magazines, videos, and commercials. Many advertisers find it necessary to splash a half-nude woman into commercials as a means to sell merchandise—because sex sells. How long must we shake our bodies and drop it like its hot? How long are we to be slaves to men and money? Has becoming a porn star or lap dancer replaced becoming a doctor or lawyer? This is a billion-dollar industry, because men see women as voluptuous, erotic goddesses. Is life only about money and power? Does power belong to a man or a woman? How many women have lost out on great opportunities because they posed in the nude? Is it worth it? What lessons did you learn from it? What would they tell teens to help them avoid exploitation?

It was not a compliment that Lynette's manager hired her on the basis of looks alone. The sad part was that she knew. Women, are we so shallow that we had to use our beauty and bodies to get ahead? Well, Lynette promised her manager that she would try to find a more creative way to gain respect from those woman-watching clowns.

Lynette did not get much of a chance to meet many of her coworkers. Most of them worked as security guards, and they were always walking the floor. On occasion, she ate lunch with some of them, and she heard about the hiding places where they went to make out. She did not indulge, not because her position did not allow it, but because her morals would not allow it. She did, however, notice one well-groomed, low-key brother in the break room. She was attracted to this young man, but she did not inquire about him, because she didn't want him to find out that she was interested.

One day as the young man made his rounds, he spotted Lynette on the elevator, and she motioned for him to come over to her. As he approached her, a sense of fear came upon her. She could have kicked herself for putting herself out there like that. As he got closer, she yelled out, "Can you bring a sista something to drink?" He looked like he was reaching for some money, and she yelled, "Oh, a sista can't get a brotha to buy her a soda?"

Embarrassed, he smiled and turned away. He immediately turned back to ask, "What kind of soda would you like to drink?" When he returned with the soda, she thanked him and offered to pay for the soda, but he declined. They engaged in small talk and properly introduced themselves. The conversation went something like this:

Him: You tried to front a brotha, ah.

Lynette: No, I was just kidding,

Him: Yeah, right.

Him: What's up with your attitude?

Lynette: What do you mean?

Him: You seem to go off on every man that approach you.

Lynette: Well, they need to learn how to respect a sista.

Him: Maybe a sista need to learn how to treat people.

Lynette: Maybe we need to end this conversation before I—

Him: Curse me out like all the rest!

As he walked away, he left Lynette with something to think about. *Why was I so upset? Why did it appear that I shut down every man who tried to be nice to me? Was I still upset about Anthony treating me like yesterday's trash? Was I punishing all men for the pain that one man had caused? Was this so-called sweet revenge turning into sour feelings, or was I justified in the way I handled those creeps?*

The only logical explanation was that Lynette was not ready to be in another committed relationship. Her first male relationship had been with her dad, and he abandoned her at the age of ten. The second most important male relationship she'd had was with Anthony. Her love had been so deep for both men that she became hurt in the process. Lynette did not know how to guide her heart away from people who could not love her in ways that would build her up. Instead she was finding relationships with men who tore her down mentally and psychologically. After suffering the trauma of a broken heart, it was hard for her to trust again.

Being in this position, Lynette felt that she was in a whirlwind of men who all wanted her for the same reason. She was a single parent, just ending a relationship with a man to whom she had devoted many years. She was paralyzed by her feelings and was operating in a mechanical state.

When a person is trying to break free from something or someone that they have been connected to for so many years, they will find it difficult to do. It's like the soul has been torn, and you are bleeding on the inside.

Lynette was grieving as if she had experienced the death of a loved one. Although Anthony was not physically dead, he had become dead to her mentally, and she could not move forward. The reason she could not be kind and courteous to anyone else was because she had not healed physically, mentally, or emotionally from the pain of her past. She was deeply wounded and needed time to nurse herself back to health.

In order to begin her healing process and successfully move on, she had to remind herself of all the terrible things Anthony had done to her. At the same time, she had to forgive herself for what she had allowed him to do to her. With each passing day, Anthony wanted to make up for all the pain he had caused. He became more attentive and spent more time with the kids to prove what a good father and man he could be if given another chance.

He was trying so hard that Lynette noticed he would do almost anything to win back the love and trust he'd once had. As a sense of revenge set in, she decided to take advantage of the opportunity. Once she realized that the control lay within her court, she grabbed it. She was going to treat Anthony the same way he had treated her for many years. Lynette would set the stage for the way their relationship was going to flow. She set the times they spent together, the places they went, and the things she wanted him to buy for her. He was solely responsible for the kids' needs as well as Lynette's. He even got an apartment for her and helped her get a new car. Things were great for her. I guess you could say she was operating in "sweet revenge."

"From now on, things will be my way or no way," she stated. "Do as I say, or you can go on your way." She thought this was the only way to protect her heart, and she vowed never again to find herself in a vulnerable state.

The next man in line would not only pay for what Anthony had done to her, but she would never open her heart again. She took Anthony back, and the difference between the old Lynette and the new Lynette was that she was the boss—demanding, assertive, and manipulative.

For centuries women had to submit to men and do what they said. As far back as 1776, the revision of the Declaration of Independence stated that "all men are created equal." The society of men interpreted that amendment in a way that did not include women. As a matter of fact, it was lawful for men to beat and mistreat their wives or partners if they got out of line. With this in mind, Lynette was about to enter into the so-called "game" that men had dominated offensively for decades. No one had ever mastered the defensive end of this "game." Now the tables had been turned, and men did not know how to guard themselves against something that they only knew in part. Lynette's sweet-and-sour defense strategy was now in motion.

Her new attitude must not have been much of a problem, because it did not stop men from asking her out. John and Lynette started hanging out, and before long, the two of them were dating. As most couples do, they shared information about their past relationships, and she made clear the things she was not going to tolerate. She was open enough to inform John that she had trust issues and would not allow any other relationship to cripple her like the first one had.

Lynette shared some information about Anthony with John. Although Anthony was not a good mate, he was a good father. "How can you separate the two?" John asked. "A good man knows how to be both." He immediately got upset because Lynette had spoken highly of Anthony as a father.

"Just because a man is not a good boyfriend or husband does not necessarily mean he cannot be a good father," Lynette explained. By no means was she going to prevent Anthony from having a relationship with his children. She had looked past his feelings and focused more on the bigger picture. Anthony's spending time with the kids gave her freedom to do whatever she wanted, and that was what she did.

On her days off, she relaxed and focused on some "me" time. Anthony had a close-knit family, and his dad was fascinated with the kids, so every year the kids spent the entire summer with their grandfather. One hot summer day as Lynette attempted to soak up some sun, a decent-looking brother stood on his porch next door. She tried not to notice him noticing her, and he didn't muster up the nerve to speak. Being a little nervous about the stares, she decided to call it a day.

The following night, as John dropped Lynette off from work, this same brother was sitting on the porch. As she approached her walkway, he told her that he had been waiting to make sure she made it home safely. He also stated that he sat on his porch every night just to watch her walk by. The funny part of this was that she had never noticed him there before. She thought to herself, *Is this man stalking me? Is he watching out for a sista, or is this brotha interested in trying to get to know me?* Whatever the case, she invited herself over to his porch for a proper introduction.

Philip was his name, and he was home from college for the summer. Philip and Lynette had a very short but wonderful conversation. She ended the night, because she had to work the next morning. He promised that he would wait up for her the following evening. Like clockwork, Philip was there each night to ensure her "safety." This situation could pose a problem. Not only was she starting to feel somewhat interested in Philip, but she was already in two other relationships with Anthony and John. She needed a strategy if she was going to continue playing this game, she thought.

If a man is interested in a woman, he is willing to do whatever it takes to get some of her time. Knowing this, Lynette was able to have a relationship with each man—with an understanding that she was not willing to commit to any of them. Each man knew that she had at least one other man, but they had no idea that there were three men involved. Each man brought something different to the table. Anthony provided for the kids, which was important, because without his assistance, she would not have had the financial support she needed to raise the kids. John provided transportation to and from work and all the extra errands she required. Philip was there for the romance. He did not have a car or a job, but he was able to give the intellectual and emotional balance she needed. You see, each man played a vital part in her life at that time, something one man alone could not have done.

A few months into this balancing act, Lynette realized that she could no longer keep up with the demands. The only reason Anthony was still around was because of her plans for sweet revenge. She was no longer in love with him, and the time she spent with him made her unavailable to spend time with the person she truly wanted to get to know.

When a person operates through revenge, it's a form of payback for pain or insult. It is defined as the act of inflicting punishment or hurt to another. Lynette's quest for revenge was not only ungodly but unforgiving. She was so determined to seek revenge that it began to eat her up on the inside like cancer.

"Do not repay anyone evil for evil. Be careful to do what is right in the eyes of everyone. If it is possible, as far as it depends on you, live at peace with everyone. Do not take revenge, my dear friends, but leave room for God's wrath, for it is written: It is mine to avenge; I will repay, says the Lord" (Romans 12:17–20 KJV).

Lynette was in a sour state of revenge, because it gave her a false sense of hope that she would feel better. But how could a person feel good about causing another to feel bad? "Do not say, 'I'll pay you back for this wrong!' Wait for the Lord and he will deliver you" (Proverbs 20:22).

When we decide to act on our own anger and bitterness, it produces revenge. When we have a "get-back" mentality, we are taking on the lordship of our own lives. This also reduces us to the same level as the people who hurt us and puts us in a place where God is not pleased with our behavior. Every vengeful act is a reminder of the hurt and pain that another person has caused you.

"For if you forgive men their trespasses, your heavenly Father will also forgive you. But if you do not forgive men their trespasses, neither will your Father forgive your trespasses" (Matthew 6:14–15 NKJV).

Lynette made a decision to let Anthony go. She knew that because of the way he had been raised, he would still be a father to his kids without being involved with her. Lynette's mom was very fond of Anthony, and because the two of them shared an apartment, Anthony had easy access to Lynette's room. She would come home, and there he would be, waiting patiently in her room. It was not that her mom hated John; she just admired Anthony for being there for his kids, which made him the family favorite. This was not good for Lynette, because it made it difficult for her to bring company home.

The summer was ending, and the kids returned home. Philip returned to school, but he left his address so that he and Lynette could keep in touch. John and Lynette attempted to spend more time together. While, Anthony took advantage of the access he had to the house, making himself comfortable, and quickly became a thorn in Lynette's side.

One night, as the three of them watched television, John's patience grew thin. He kindly invited Anthony into the kitchen to talk. One thing led to another, and before long, the two were wrestling in the kitchen. Lynette and her mom had to pull the two of them apart, and her mom motioned for John to leave. Lynette quickly defended him, shouting at her mom, "If you want Anthony to stay, he will have to go to your room, not mine!" Lynette needed to form an understanding with her mom that her relationship with Anthony was over. She also had to remind her mom about all the things this man had put her through. She said she would no longer come home and find him in her room. She felt that if he wanted to see the kids, he could pick them up and take them with him.

After all the rude treatment Lynette had dished out toward Anthony, he finally gave up. This was great news for her, because she would finally be able to have a real relationship without falsehoods or distractions.

Lynette's manager pulled her off her assignment as elevator operator and made her a security guard. She thought that if she was performing more work, she should get more pay. In this case, since she was making more money than the others, it was considered a lateral move. Lynette did not like this position because it required much standing and walking. John tried to show her the fun that he found in the job, but she was not pleased with the switch, so she started looking for a new job.

John had a friend named Ty who started spending time with them. Everywhere they went, this man followed. Lynette was getting a bit disturbed by their relationship, and she asked this brother, "Do you have a girlfriend?" There had been times when Ty and John had disappeared, leaving her sitting alone, and waiting for what felt like hours. What were the ties between the two men? John lived in the west suburbs, his friend lived on the south side of town, they worked for two different companies, and they had not grown up together or attended the same school. What was the connection? Why, after all this time, had John never mentioned this friend to Lynette? Something about their relationship just did not seem right, and Lynette was determined to find the truth. She could not pinpoint what it was about this dude that she did not like.

John and Lynette conversed about it, and he convinced her that she was being overly analytical. She later found out that Ty lived on the same block as John's aunt. One day while visiting the aunt, Lynette and John ran into Ty and his girlfriend. *Why is this the first time I've seen her?* Lynette wondered.

After spending some time with John's aunt, he decided to pay Ty a visit. It was a dark, small, and smelly place. Lynette could barely see her hands in front of her face. In a joking manner, she whispered, "A brotha didn't pay his light bill." Apparently she did not whisper softly enough, because Ty heard her and replied, "My bills are paid. I just like the ambience."

After a long silence, Ty handed John what looked like marijuana, but it had an unusual smell. John puffed and tried to pass it to Lynetter. She quickly declined and asked, "What are you smoking? It has a funny smell." The three of them laughed, ignoring the question. As the girlfriend quickly nodded off, John leaned over and said to Lynette, "I'll be right back." He and Ty excused themselves from the room, leaving her alone.

What was going on? Was she the only leveled-headed, sober person around? Her blood was boiling, and she could not wait to get out of there. She did not know what was going on, but she felt that if this place was raided, they would all go to jail. On the way home, John got to see the worst side of Lynette. She sounded like a drunken sailor. She was so upset that she did not see John for weeks. If fact, the situation drew her back to Anthony, a familiar place. She was not sure what was going on. All she knew was that she hated her job and that her relationship with John was very questionable.

Ty informed John that the company he worked for was hiring, and if Lynette was interested, he would put in a good word for her. Was this John's way of getting back in Lynette's good graces? She never questioned him about that day at Ty's home, as part of her did not want to know and the other part did not care. She started a new job, processing credit applications for a retail appliance store, and all was well. Right!

One day John and Lynette were in her room, watching TV, and her mom kept walking back and forth, singing a song. The hook to the song was, "You gonna have to face it, you're addicted to love," but dear old mother had put a twist on the lyrics by singing, "Gonna have to face it, you're addicted to drugs." She went on and on, and Lynette, thinking her mom just had the lyrics mixed up, decided to correct her.

Lynette's mom boldly told her that she could sing the song any way she chose. It was not until the next day that Lynette realized that her mom was sending a subliminal message to John. She informed Lynette that John's brother had paid her a visit the day before. He had told her that John was on drugs and Ty was his drug dealer, and that he was concerned for Lynette's safety. Months after this, John moved back to his hometown, where he later died of a cocaine overdose.

I would like to add a side bar to talk about these lyrics:

Your lights are on, but you're not home.
Your mind is not your own.
Your heart sweats, your body shakes.
Another kiss is what it takes.

Lynette was naive and did not know anything about using drugs or their effects. The lyrics of this song clearly depict signs and symptoms of drug addiction. What can consume a person to the point that he or she can live life without consciousness? What will alter adrenaline and cause the heart to race and the body to quiver? What is that thing you crave or desire and devote all your time and energy trying to obtain? What have you tried to fight off and resist? What is in your life that you have grown weak to?

If there are some significant changes in the behavior and attitude of a person, it could be that this person is on drugs. Lynette did not know John when he first started using drugs, so she did not know that his behavior was unusual. Each drug causes specific symptoms, but the most common ones are those described in the song.

Facts: Forty to fifty percent of high school students will try some form of drug, even manufacturing ways of getting high from cleaning products at home. Marijuana is still the most commonly used drug. It was used by 7 percent of Americans in 2011. The number of people who reported heroin use in the past year rose from 373,000 in 2007 to 620,000 in 2011. Between 2006 and 2011, there were reductions in reported past-month use of cocaine (44 percent) and methamphetamine (40 percent). There was a 19 percent decrease in past-month use of hallucinogens between 2010 and 2011. For more information, visit *US News Health*: health.usnews.com/health-news/news/articles/2012/09/24/prescription-drug-abuse-drops-among-us-young-adults.

Some things to look out for in drug users are dilated pupils (larger or smaller than usual), a blank stare, watery eyes, loss of appetite, awake at unusual times, difficulty paying attention, excessive sweating, sweaty palms, shaky hands, runny nose, hacking, and sniffing. The song speaks about something you love so much that without it, your body would have withdrawal symptoms.

We might as well face it: we are all addicted to something. The affect of it may start out sweet, but in the end, it will leave us sour. This chapter was a point in Lynette's life when she would not allow Anthony to move past what he had done. Therefore, they were both "in prison." He was the perpetrator of the crime, and she was the gatekeeper of the prison, making sure he did not escape the actions that had caused her pain. This is not the way God intended for His people to behave. We are to let go and allow God to heal us and mature us in spiritual matters. Sometimes things happen because God is pruning us.

If you are operating in revenge, retaliation, or resentment, ask God to help you operate in forgiveness. Ask for forgiveness so that you can be set free, delivered from past hurts and pain. Ask God to help you release the people who inflicted the hurt and pain so that they will no longer control your emotions and your life.

"Vengeance is Mine, and recompense. Their foot shall slip in due time; for the day of their calamity is at hand. And the things to come hasten upon them" (Deuteronomy 32:35).

CHAPTER 4

Kryptonite: The Death of Superman

And he said unto me, My grace is sufficient for thee: for my strength
is made perfect in weakness. Most gladly therefore will I rather
glory in my infirmities, that the power of Christ may rest upon me.
—2 Corinthians 12:9

Superman—the "man of steel," the one who was able to leap tall buildings in a single bound, who was faster than a speeding bullet, who was more powerful than a locomotive—had a weakness: *kryptonite!* The mere thought of this substance entering into his system would render him powerless. Once Superman allowed kryptonite to overtake him, it would drop this invincible man to his knees and eventually take his life. Just like Superman, we all struggle at some point with something that causes us to fall, leaving us feeling defenseless against its attack.

Note: Satan knows your weaknesses or sin, because these are the same things that have hindered and attacked generations before you.

Weakness is defined as "lacking physical strength and energy," and it causes us to crack under pressure or stress. Whether the cause of weakness is drugs, sex, stealing, cheating, or lying, we all struggle in some area. Lynette's biggest weakness or struggle was twofold: men and sex. Now, you may say that the two go hand-in-hand, but there is a difference between loving the pleasure and being a nymphomaniac. Although both are sinful, nymphomaniacs are so hyper in their elevated desire for sex that it becomes problematic, affecting their daily activities in the same way as drugs and alcohol. It is a clinical condition that includes the concept of high levels of desire or activity that cause addiction or compulsivity. When a nymphomaniac gets involved in threesomes, makes videos or movies, or is just a "girl gone wild," there is an absence of the love and emotions that God intended for marriage. Sex becomes impersonal, lacking intimacy, and this person can never be satisfied.

We may know of people who have been lured into immorality or promiscuity. Lynette was not exempt from sin, weakness, or failure. I am not sure what made her defenseless, but like Superman, she had some mechanism in her that made her vulnerable. What was God's purpose in telling us to keep ourselves for marriage? Was He being "mean" and trying to keep us from having fun?

I know one thing, Lynette thought to herself. *I wish I had waited!* Because of sin, she had created powerful bonds with men who were abusive, manipulative, and unkind. She had not intended to have such relationships, but because she had not been aware of all the consequences of partaking in premarital sex, she had become a promiscuous girl, a teenage mother, a single parent, and a victim of rape and domestic violence.

She did not know that, while indulging in this sin, she would experience date rape and stalking when she said no. She did not know that she would have black eyes and a busted nose because of this one thing. She was not aware that sin would take her further than she wanted to go. She did not know that she was setting up her children for a fatherless, broken home and a life of failed relationships. If only I had been able to warn her, she would have known that abortions cause lifetime scars and that sex does not secure a place in a man's heart. She would have known that living life recklessly would cause her to live in constant fear of pregnancy and

STDs. If I could have reached out to young Lynette, I would have been able to tell her that her adversary, the devil was setting her up for failure.

In my psychology classes, I studied the principles of careful observation, as they relate to emotional and behavioral characteristics. William James, a psychologist and philosopher, believed that psychology should study how our minds function to adapt to our changing environment. John B. Watson, who was often referred to as the father of behaviorism, thought that psychology should be concerned with the study of human behavior, not the mind. Carl Rogers and Abraham Maslow, taking the humanistic approach, emphasized the role of "sense of self" or the "human being" and felt that human beings could freely choose to live as they wanted.

If I'd had to give Lynette a diagnosis of her condition, I would have stated that her mind was conditioned to adapt to her environment, causing the behavior of choosing freely to live as she pleased. I would conclude that, because she had missed out on love and confirmation from her father, she was looking to have it replaced by other means—men. She had never been told that she was beautiful or that she was loved, so when guys spoke these idle words to her, she melted like butter on a piece of hot toast. These attributes should have already been established in her. She couldn't count the number of times a man had told her that he was attracted to her. There was no way to describe the number of times she had been told she had beautiful eyes a great body or a wonderful smile. It was the same old line, used by a different man on any given day.

The sad part about it was that these idle words worked every time for every man. If she was lucky, she received a combination of all four lines in one day. She had to admit that she loved the attention, even though it was empty and meaningless. Just hearing those words made her feel good, special, important, admired, and pretty. This behavior is known as *classical conditioning*. It is an unconditioned response: the same impetus always gets the same result. It is a natural response to the unconditioned stimulus. When a man told Lynette these things, they acted as an automatic trigger. Think about it: when you smell good cooking, even if you are not hungry, your mouth starts to water, and you can hardly wait to dig in.

"Let them lay aside every weight and the sin which so easily besets us, and let them run with patience the race that is set before us" (Hebrews 12:1b NKJV).

Lynette was living a life of sin. Sinning means that you have crossed the boundary line set by God. It puts you in a foul zone, one that causes loss and grief. If you have ever played any sports, you know that the court or field has a designated playing ground or playing area. This tells you that any action beyond the lines is considered foul play. Once a player crosses the line, he has committed an offense, and a penalty is called against him. In the game of life, what consequence are you paying for because you stepped out of bounds? What ungodly substance or sin has a noose around your neck and is leading you across the boundary line?

You walk around, pretending to be something you are not. Trying to keep your sin a secret, you get up every morning, posing as a God-fearing person, a good parent, a wholesome teacher, or even a preacher, but deep down inside, you are nothing more than a sinner. You dress up in your business attire, hold board meetings, and run mega million-dollar companies, and yet there is something that has the same grip on you that kryptonite had on Superman. Each and every person—yes, even you—has had something that bond you. At any given time, this thing can choke the very life out of you, because you are not strong enough to fight against its attack.

What if you were incarcerated right now for that thing you do only in the dark, at night, while everyone is asleep—you know, that thing you do when no one is watching that you're sure no one will ever catch you doing? Confess! I've heard that it's good for the soul. This may be your chance to be set free. Think of that one thing you cannot live without, that addiction, that habit—yes, that thing right there! It could be an ungodly relationship. It could be adultery, gambling, drugs, lying, or stealing. What is it? The Bible tells us that "all have sinned and come short of the glory of God." What is your sin, weakness, lust, habit, or vice?

This is not to say that kryptonite was Superman's *sin*. It is only used as an example to show that no matter how strong you are, the Devil will use that ungodly thing, that sin hidden deep in your heart, for your demise. Ungodliness happens when you place anything or anyone above your relationship with God. It occurs when you allow something other than Christ to control or guide you to the degree that you lust after it and will lie to get it. Ungodliness occurs when you will forsake something important to get that thing. This is a sin against God. If this sounds familiar and you are behaving this way, you are in an ungodly relationship.

The addiction and attraction of this sin is so strong that even if you wanted to stop, you wouldn't know how, because the call of it is much louder and greater than the call God has for your life. *Addiction* is defined as "devoting or giving oneself to something habitually or compulsively." God has placed in all of us a certain measure of power. In spite of the fight in you or your natural powers, you will always have at least one thing that will challenge you. That powerful thing is similar to kryptonite. It weakens you to the point of sinning, and when sin is completed, it brings about death

According to Romans 3:23,we all stumble in many things. As we strive for perfection in every aspect of our lives, we will make mistakes. We err in our choices, our judgment, our faith, and even in our dedication to God, but we cannot afford to be overtaken or caught up in our mistakes and sin.

"Let the words of my mouth and the meditation of my heart be acceptable in thy sight, O LORD, my rock and my redeemer" (Psalm 19:14).

Hear ye, hear ye, all you liars. Incline your ears to the Word of the Lord. Liars will not enter into the kingdom of God. The Bible talks about lying and its relation to deceit, betrayal, misleading, beguiling, and deluding. This one sin has caused society to deteriorate. Many innocent people are incarcerated because of a "little white lie." All sin is dangerous, and the sooner we learn, the sooner we can begin to do better. And when we do better, we are better able to please God.

"Now the works of the flesh are manifest, which are these; adultery, fornication, uncleanness, lasciviousness, idolatry, witchcraft, hatred, variance, emulations, wrath, strife, seditions, heresies, envyings, murders, drunkenness, revellings, and such like: of the which I tell you before, as I have also told you in time past, that we which do such things shall not inherit the kingdom of God (Galatians 5:19–21).

Olly olly oxen, free, free, free! This is a call to those who are bound in the ungodly act of adultery and fornication to come and be liberated. Both adultery and fornication are unlawful acts. They are like kryptonite and will hinder your walk with God. The Bible warns us that those who continue a lifestyle of fornication and adultery will not inherit God's kingdom. God created intimacy to be a blessing of the union between a husband and wife. He clearly and absolutely disapproves of all other parameters. Society has accepted fornication and adultery, and same-gender relationships are considered normal. That is a trick of the Enemy. Whether we are Christians or not yet saved, we need to recognize how our souls and spirits are affected after this behavior. The Bible teaches that we should have control over our members, and because many people cannot control their urges, women and children are abused.

"Blessed is the man that endureth temptation: for when he is tried, he shall receive the crown of life, which the Lord hath promised to them that love him. Let no man say when he is tempted, I am tempted of God: for God cannot be tempted with evil, neither tempteth he any man: but every man is tempted, when he is drawn away of his own lust, and enticed.

Then when lust hath conceived, it bringeth forth sin: and sin, when it is finished, bringeth forth death" (James 1:12–15).

This is a call to parents, grandparents, step-parents, godparents, and the like: *stop bailing grown kids out of jail!* You spend countless hours praying and interceding for them, acting as their "super hero," while they are out there doing whatever they want to do, even when they know it's against the law. Once you bail them out of jail, they go back to doing the same things. They have no legal job, yet they come into your home wearing designer clothes and bling-bling, rolling on dubs. They hide drugs and guns in your house, and without notice, the police raid your home, looking for Ray Ray. Not only are you at risk of losing the house that you worked so hard to get, but you spend your entire retirement bailing "baby boy" out of jail. No wonder you cannot retire. You are working for Ray Ray.

To all you girlfriends and baby mommies, stop playing "Rescue Ranger" to these good-for-nothing mama's boys. You have not heard from Pooky for days, weeks, or even months. Once he gets locked up, he remembers your phone number. You get up in the middle of the night, leaving your babies at home unattended or dragging them out of bed to go get him. You take your rent money to bail him out, and once he is released, he disappears—just like Houdini. Now you have to go to each court appearance, because you don't want to lose your bail money.

Wonder Woman, stop letting Tyrone live with you while he is on house arrest. He did not want you when he was acting like a baller, thinking he'd "made it" on the street to the "big time." But now that he needs your help, he finally realizes what a good woman you are. When superheroes find trouble, they eliminate it. They do not harbor the fugitives.

"If we confess our sins, he is faithful and just to forgive us our sins, and to cleanse us from all unrighteousness" (1 John 1:9).

Thank God that He will expunge your record of sin when you confess, repent, and turn from your wicked ways. Whatever it is that has kept you down in the past, choose this day to make that change. Do not let kryptonite cripple you any longer. I pray that you no longer allow the works of the flesh and your disobedience to God be the death of you!

CHAPTER 5

Checkmate: Adam, Where Art Thou?

And the Lord God said, "It is not good that man should be alone.
I will make him a helper comparable to him."
—Genesis 2:18

God took a rib from a man and formed a woman to become his helpmate. If God felt that it was not good for the man to be alone, where did current societal thinking get the idea that the woman could raise the kids without help? In the first book of the Bible, Adam allowed Eve to fend for herself when the Serpent approached her in the garden of Eden. He just stood idly by, watching. His role was to lead, provide, and protect. Adam, I know you were there. Why did you not stand up for your wife? Why did you let the snake slither its way into your home and sweet-talk your Eve? You were supposed to be the head and the spiritual leader of the home. What happened?

In this context, Adam represents the husbands and fathers of the home, and they are responsible for taking care of the family. But where art thou, Adam? You play a very important role in raising your children, but *where art thou*? When God asked Adam, "Where art thou?," it was not a question that God didn't have the answer to. He wanted Adam to assert his position in his home. God wanted Adam to look around and recognize his own state of mind and well-being.

The moment Adam ate from the forbidden tree, he and Eve realized that they were naked and became ashamed. In this passage, the word _naked_ means "to be without." They were no longer innocent, and that was why they tried to cover themselves, causing them to be without a covering. Sin took them away from the protection of God, and the source of their shame was disobedience. Jeremiah 51 says that every man is made stupid by knowledge because of his limitations. That is why the Bible instructs us to get understanding. Adam blamed Eve for their sin, and people continue to blame others for their actions. So Adam, where were you, and why are you still hiding?

In the game of chess, _check_ is defined as being placed in a position where winning is almost impossible and escaping is not easy. As in the game of chess, being "in check" in life places a person in a position of potential defeat. It is used metaphorically to show that someone has been removed from his protective position, thus leaving others vulnerable. This is what happens with husbands and fathers leave home. Their families are open for the negative consequences of not having the love, support, respect, and guidance of their Adam. In the game of chess, when you are in checkmate, the game is considered over. In life, serious struggles begin to take their toll on the mother and children.

Facts: Sixty-three percent of youth suicides are from fatherless homes (US Department of Health/Census). Ninety percent of all homeless and runaway children are from fatherless homes. Eighty-five percent of all children who show behavior disorders come from fatherless homes (Centers for Disease Control). Eighty percent of rapists with anger problems come from fatherless homes (_Criminal Justice and Behavior_, no. 14, 403–426). For more on "the fatherless generation," visit TheFatherlessGeneration. wordpress.com/statistics/.

Lynette's father thought he was doing his thing whenever he dropped by and gave her a dollar or two. Her father had _really_ left when she was about ten. I use the phrase _"really_ left," because he was already gone emotionally, financially, and spiritually. When he was home, he was only home physically. He did not spend much sober time at home, so Lynette felt that he had been gone long before he picked up and moved out. Her mom did the best she could do, but there are just some things a little girl need from her daddy.

Fathers, you can bring virtuousness back to your little girls—if you stop being so selfish and stop your neurotic behavior. You are the role models for your daughters, and you have a responsibility to cherish, love, and support them. You set the stage for the way they see men and whether or not they will be treated well and respected. Your daughters' relationships with men will be patterned after what they have received from you, and if their experiences are negative, this will cause their relationships with other men to fail.

Lynette's first husband was just like her father. In her eyes, her father was an alcoholic, and so was her husband. Her father spent most of his time on the street doing his thing, and her husband did the same. Her father would come home drunk and tried to abuse her mom, and her husband tried the same thing.

If I had known then what I know now, I would have told Lynette not to marry that man. But Lynette was so determined to guard herself from the attacks her mom had endured that she left an area of her life unprotected. She ended up in relationships with men who had the same traits as her father.

The reason her relationships had failed, the reason she did not trust men and looked for love in all the wrong places, was that she had been put into "checkmate" when her father left the "board." A girl faces checkmate when her father, who represents the king, removes himself from her life. When he does so, she is at risk for failure in relationships and other areas. For too long, fathers have disappeared from the lives of their biological children.

Fact: When children lack a dad or dad-like figure in their lives, they are at a higher risk for suicide, substance abuse, teen pregnancy, incarceration, and homelessness.

Lynette's father cannot hear her now, but I can speak on behalf of many sons and daughters: "Dad, they need you! They need your love, your support, and your protection. Daddy, they need your guidance to help them understand who they are and to teach them how to be appreciated and validated as little girls."

Lynette was a single parent, and her daughters approached her many times with questions she could not answer: Mommy, why does Daddy always lie to us? Why won't Daddy return our calls? Do you think he's coming to pick us up this time? Mommy, why does Daddy spend more time with her kids and not with us? Mommy, why does Daddy act like he doesn't love us?

There were plenty of nights when Lynette's daughters fell asleep at the window, waiting for their dad to pick them up. There were plenty of nights when her daughters cried themselves to sleep, because dear, old dad had lied again. Her daughters' relationships with men were in danger of being sabotaged because of their poor, inexcusable relationship with the first man in their lives—their *daddy*.

If I had known then what I know now, I would have prayed and asked God to break the curses over Lynette and many others like her, so their daughters would not be in potential danger of "checkmate." I would have known that God would be a replacement for their earthly fathers. He would have been their comforter during the many nights that they cried. If only I had known that God said in His Word that He would be a father to the fatherless, then I would have known that God would answer my prayers concerning those mothers and daughters in their time of need. God would have stepped in and helped them make critical decisions, even in their youth, that would have kept them out of "checkmate."

The family structure is like the game of chess. The object in chess is to checkmate the king. Checkmate, or just *mate*, occurs when a king is attacked and cannot escape capture. The game of life is also lost, if the man resigns or gives up because the situation looks hopeless. Satan has a trap to destroy the entire family unit. He starts with capturing the piece that seems the easiest or weakest, which in most cases happens to be the husband and father. In the game of life, the king is not the only target. The wife, or queen, also holds royal status. Destroy her and you kill mankind. The bishop and rook symbolize our children. Destroy them, and you destroy the future.

In regular chess, it is illegal for a man to move in any direction that will let his royal piece be open for possible capture. If this is true for chess, why is it so easy in life for the "king" to walk out on his family? Why are so many men of the "DL"? ("Down low" are married men who sleep with other men privately.) Why are jails overcrowded with our "kings"? Although the game would be considered over in chess, life application has just begun. The Devil will not stop until he has destroyed the entire family structure.

Lynette was forced to take care of her daughters by herself. As she adapted to being the head, she had to work two jobs to support her family. She had to take money from her car note to pay the light bill. She had to decide what was more important—medication or food. She was full of resentment and hatred toward her father and the father of her children, because she and her mom had been left with all the responsibilities of parenting. All you real dads, step-dads, godfathers, and big brothers—we salute you. Some of us would not have made it without your support. But there is no substitute for the love, involvement, and commitment of the biological parents in a child's life.

Like our predecessor Adam, our men today are still playing hide-and-seek. The question, "Adam, where art thou?," was not intended to learn Adam's geographical location. It was intended to mean, "What caused you to leave?" So many women and children need to know what caused their husbands and fathers to leave home and abdicate the head-of-house position that God had given them. What caused them to jump ship and abandon their families? Where are they now? Why are they playing father and husband to someone else's child, while being a deadbeat dad to their own?

If the "king" had not been absent from Lynette's home, she would not have been attacked in many facets of her life. Instead, she was placed in checkmate, time and time again; even as she hoped that one day her knight in shining armor would come. If only she'd had her father to teach her to love and respect herself, then maybe she would have required this same behavior from the men in her life. She would have expected men to cherish her like her dad had cherished her. She would not have fallen for the same old lines about how beautiful and sexy she was. She would have already known that she possessed those traits and would have made guys treat her more honorably. She would not have felt the pressure to have sex just because a man had taken her out on a cheap date.

Are you a missing or an absentee dad? Are you on the "deadbeats most wanted list"? If you are a delinquent dad, there is no time like the present to get involved in your child's life. When will you stop being a fugitive? Don't you think your kid has suffered and waited long enough? Don't you think it is time for you to become the man of God that you were called to be? Let your daughters, as well as your sons, know how it feels to be loved and cherished. Show them that they are to be respected. Take them to nice restaurants, and be the first man to buy your daughter diamond earrings. Open car doors and pull out chairs for them. Chivalry is not dead. It is just forgotten.

Fathers, when you pick up your little girls, do not honk your horn for them. Get out of the car, ring the bell, and escort them to the car. If you show your little girls how beautiful they are and validate their worth, the knuckleheads that will approach them will not blow their minds with small talk, and your daughters will no longer fall for the "Okee-Doke" (slick talk).

Ladies, we are to pray for the men in our lives—and in the lives of our daughters. We are not leaving our sons out, because they need their dads too. So, as we stand in the gap for our "kings," let's not forget the royal priesthood that is our sons. We are praying for our husbands, boyfriends, fiancés, baby daddies, sons, and sons-in-law to be the men God has called them to be. We are praying against deadbeat dads, absentee dads, teenage dads, abusiveness, alcoholism, drug addiction and irresponsible fathers. We call men to be more devoted, loving, and caring—in the name of Jesus.

I pray that our daughters will not allow their first bad experience with a man named "Dad" to dictate what all their relationships with men will be like. I bind every generational curse; every plot, scheme, and demise the Devil has against our daughters as it relates to men. May our daughters be set free from looking for affection from men, knowing that Jesus has already validated their worth on the cross.

Men, you will respect our daughters, and they will treat them like the queens they are. Fathers, you will step up to the plate and support your daughters mentally, emotionally, and financially and more importantly, spiritually. You will no longer hide from your responsibilities as the father and protector over the lives of your children.

For every person who suffers from the negative effects of fatherlessness, I decree that you are delivered from any and all social problems, the need to look for love from others, the spirit of rejection, rebellion, and any other behavior resulting from the absence of your fathers. I pray that you will no longer act like victims, just because of your fatherless childhoods. All these things I ask in Jesus' name, amen!

"But ye are a chosen generation, a royal priesthood, an holy nation, a peculiar people; that ye should shew forth the praises of him who hath called you out of darkness into his marvellous light" (1 Peter 2:9).

CHAPTER 6

The Wardrobe for Battle: Bring It On!

An angry man stirreth up strife, and a furious
man aboundeth in transgression.
—Proverbs 29:22–24

Growing up in the early to mid seventies, Lynette was approached many times to join a gang. Fortunately for her, someone had already claimed her at a very young age. In her day, the original street gangs were Folk Nation, People Nation, Black Gangster Disciples, and Vice-Lords. In order to be identified with a particular gang, members adopted certain colors and wore certain types of clothing, tattoos, and hairstyles. Graffiti on walls of buildings also identified whose territory or neighborhood you were in.

At the age of twelve, Lynette was not sure why she had been chosen to join this specific gang. All she knew about them was that once you were in, you were in for life. She had heard about the protection this gang provided and that she could call on the members of this family to help her in any situation. Lynette figured that since she was spending so much time with these people, she might as well participate and enjoy the benefits of what her new family had to offer.

She too had to wear a certain type of gear so that she could represent the group she was down with. She had to suit up every day, and if she did not properly represent, her enemies could attack her at any time—or worse, kill her. She had to learn what all the parts of her gear symbolized and how to apply or activate them in case of an ambush. There were many helpful rules and regulations to follow, and if you belonged to a gang, you had to learn all the laws and commandments so you wouldn't violate your "commander in chief." The leader of the gang was not your run-of-the-mill, average Joe. He was and still is known as "Lord of Lords" and "King of Kings."

Lynette later found out that she was in the oldest, most beloved and legal gang there was. She was, and still is, a part of the "Disciples of Jesus." Their dress code is called "the whole armor of God."

Lynette's grandmother took her to church every Sunday from the time she was about twelve years old. She was also baptized in the name of the Father, Son, and Holy Ghost. Her grandmother was a pillar of the church, and therefore, much was required of Lynette as well. Lynette sang in the choir, and she even formed a singing group with her four sisters. Each Sunday and each service, her group was on the program to sing. They were forced to attend Baptist Training Union (B.T.U), morning service, evening service, night service, choir rehearsal, Bible study, and everything else her grandmother could drag them to.

Back then, people did not have a relationship with God; rather, they were into religion. Religion is a set of beliefs and rules that cannot be changed or altered. It is a systemic operation that ran on agendas, time frames, and programs. There was no such thing as "free flow" or being moved by the Spirit of God. There was no room in the service for that. If, by chance, they allotted "shout" time, Sister Betsy, who was known to shout too long, was removed from the service for disruption, because it didn't take all that. There was no speaking in tongue, healing, deliverance, or prophecy. These things were not on the program. There was no youth ministry, youth leader, or children's church; the entire congregation learned at the same level. You dared not ask questions during Bible class, or you would be pulled out, reprimanded, and viewed as a troublemaker. Church members served, worshipped, and honored the men or women of the church, not God.

"Study to shew thyself approved unto God, a workman that needeth not to be ashamed, rightly dividing the word of truth" (2 Timothy 2:15 KJV).

God is relational. He desires to have a close connection with us. According to Genesis 3, God made time for Adam and Eve. He walked with them in the garden. He talked with them. He had a personal, intimate relationship with them. When you have a real relationship with someone, you consider that person and include them in everything. You want to know what's on his/her mind, their likes and dislikes. You study them to see what sets them off, what makes them happy. You think of ways to nature, maintain, and show this person how much you care. You would do almost anything to sustain this relationship with that person. You think about him/her day and night. You fall asleep on the phone with the person, because you didn't want the night to end.

God is no different. We need to talk with Him, read His Word, show outwardly that we are in love with Him, tell others about Him, and get to know His heartbeat. We need to get involved, get connected, and get to know God.

As Lynette got older, she started paying more attention to the sermons being preached. She took notes, trying to understand the subject at hand. The only message, sermon, or teaching that took her years to understand was how to put on the full armor of God. If she had known then what she knows now about the full armor of God, she would have been more prepared and equipped to defend herself in the time of battle. She would have prayed more over her thoughts and would have had the mind of Christ Jesus (Philippians 2:5). She would have guarded her heart with all diligence (Proverbs 4:23). She would have asked God to order her steps, because a good man's steps are ordered by the Lord (Psalm 37:23). She would have prayed that she would always speak the truth (John 17:17). If only she had known.

As a soldier in God's army, where is your uniform? Why are you leaving the house underdressed and unequipped? You will never see a basketball player on the court in a business suit and a pair of gaiters trying to play ball. Such a player would be totally unprepared to play in the game. Even if the player was a bench member and his chances of getting in the game were slim to none, he would still suit up properly. If umpires or referees were not dressed properly, they would not only be powerless, but they would be just another person on the field or court. They would also risk the chance of being tackled by players, attacked by fans or arrested by police for being out of place.

You will never see firefighters in the midst of a fire trying to put on their boots, helmets, and masks. Instead, they leave the station prepared for their assignment. Police officers would never go to a call without being in uniform and carrying their guns. They too go prepared for the situation.

So, why are you leaving your house without having on the armor of God? The armor of God defends you against the schemes and attacks of the Enemy, and it defeats him as well. Imagine yourself being called to active duty in the United States Army, being on the battlefield, and not knowing how to use your weaponry. Well, that is what a Christian does every day when he stays ignorant of the Word of God!

We all desire compliments from others, that is why we spend way too much time in front of the mirror, putting on our Lancôme makeup, trying to decide on which purse today Dolce & Gabbana or Coach. God is not impressed with your outerwear, and the Devil is not threatened by it. What matters most is how you dress spiritually. Leaving the house as an "undressed" Christian puts you at risk of defeat by the Enemy. In

Ephesians 6:11–17, the apostle Paul encourages and instructs us to put on the "whole armor of God."

Knowing what to put on is one thing; knowing how to use the pieces is the key to survival. The armor alone has no power to defeat the Devil, but when it is linked with the power of God—just like the young superheroes, the Wonder Twins—the armor can activate our powers. By being connected with God and the things of God, He communicates with us through the telepathic power of His Word, and through prayer, He instantly alerts us of trouble.

Knowing how to activate our armor will help us withstand in these last, evil days. The Greek word for *withstand* is "*anthistemi,*" which tells us to be vigorous in our fight against the Enemy—to be brave, to resist defection, to stand our ground against the adversary. We have the authority of Christ, and He grants us spiritual weapons so that we, as Christians, can survive all the evil forces that attempt to attack us daily.

"And take the helmet of salvation" (Ephesians 6:17 NKJV).

The "helmet of salvation" is known as the "hope of deliverance." The helmet protects our heads, because it is in our minds that the war is raging. The mind is also known to be the battleground or playground. The Devil will try to deposit thoughts in our minds to commit sin. If the Devil can kidnap our minds, he has control over us. The Greek word for *salvation* is "*soterion.*" This is the experience of deliverance given by God to anyone who accepts His Son, Jesus Christ.

Through salvation, Jesus extends peace to the one who accepts Him, and He imparts wisdom through hope in Him. Renewing the mind is the first process for using the helmet. The mind must be saved and transformed from what the world has done to it (the old way of thinking) to what God originally planned for it. We have hope in knowing God, and He will deliver us. Salvation will renew our ways of thinking, and we will begin to live life without sin and condemnation.

"And be not conformed to this world: but be ye transformed by the renewing of your mind, that ye may prove what is that good, and acceptable, and perfect, will of God (Romans 12:2).

God fashioned the skull to protect the brain from hurt, harm, and danger. When there is a blow to the head, the skull acts as a cushion. This is the same way the helmet works when we are hit spiritually. The helmet not only softens the attack to our minds, but the helmet prevents it from penetrating our thoughts. The mind is located in the brain, and one of its functions is to identify reality. The brain holds our intellect and emotions in response to what the mind perceives as real, and this dictates our behavior. When we put on the helmet of salvation, it simply means that we pray to God to deliver us from sin, and He protects our minds from being captured by the Devil.

The key word in the name of this piece of armor is *salvation*. We all need deliverance from our own destructive actions and from the negative thoughts that have been planted in our minds. Since salvation is the major theme in this passage of Scripture, wearing the helmet of salvation leaves no room for a defeated mind-set. We no longer have to live apart from God. We can get set today.

The simple plan of salvation is to confess with our mouths the Lord Jesus and to believe in our hearts that God has raised Jesus from the dead—and we shall be saved. For with the heart a man believes unto righteousness, and with the mouth, confession is made unto salvation (Romans 10:9–10). It's just that simple. And a born-again Christian should never again leave the house without putting on his helmet so that his salvation is protected and he can begin living a victorious life.

"Stand therefore, having girded your waist with truth" (Ephesians 6:14a NKJV).

Satan is the Father of Lies, and there is no such thing as a "little white lie"! We say things like, "I just said that because I did not want to hurt your feelings" or "I did not think you could handle the truth." Satan uses the tactic of small lies so that he can appear to you as an angel of light. You need to recognize the truth so that you can spot the lies the Devil brings your way. Telling the truth will set you free from the consequences and backlash of a false statement. We should know the truth about sin, its consequences, the attacks of the Enemy, and the power of God.

When Paul instructed us in the book of Ephesians to have our loins girt about with truth (also referred to as the "belt of truth"), he was telling us not to secure or tie up anything around us that will cause us to lie and fall, including omission and false witnessing. The Greek word for *truth* is "*alethinos*," which means to speak truthfully and to have a sense of "genuine things" and sincerity in the heart. Because your loins are located at your pelvis, girding your loins protects your reproductive system. Therefore, you are to reproduce truth—or Jesus, who is the absolute truth.

When we speak to people, they should know that what we are saying is direct, real, and good for consumption. It is not a lie but the truth! One of Satan's weapons is distortion of the truth. He is a deceiver and will try to keep us in a state of confusion by twisting the Word of God. The loins of a human or quadruped are located on either side of the backbone, between the ribs and hips. Since you have a backbone, stand up for truth. You should walk in truth, hold truth in your belly, and produce truth at all times.

"Jesus saith unto him, 'I am the way, the truth, and the life: no man cometh unto the Father, but by me" (John 14:6).

Truth is the key word here. We all know that Satan is the Father of Lies and that he has always deceived God's people about the power of God, the consequences of sin, our identity in Christ, and the effectiveness of prayer. When we allow Satan or sin to rule our lives, our belt is corrupted, because there is no truth in us. To wear our belt each day, we must speak truthfully, study the Word, and pray that God would remind us of what is true.

A good illustration is a movie entitled *Wanted*, starring Morgan Freeman and Angelina Jolie. It is about a fraternity of assassins who recruited a wimpy, twenty-five-year-old man named Wes. This young man was living his life, believing that he would never amount to anything. He was slapped around because he did not know who he was. He was recruited by the group of assassins when they tricked him into thinking that his father had been brutally murdered and that he needed to be trained to avenge his father's death. What the group of killers failed to realize was that Wes carried the DNA of his father, which made him a gifted assassin.

How many of us can identify with Wes? We are bullied and tossed around by the Devil, because we, just like Wes, do not know the truth about who we are and the power that we have—because we have the DNA of Jesus. The message in this movie showed me that a person can reestablish his power, by knowing and believing what God says about us. We must stop being victims of identity fraud and take back control over our lives in Christ.

After Jesus fasted for forty days and nights, he was tired and hungry. Satan tried to entice Jesus to sin (Matthew 4). From a Christian perspective, Jesus showed us in this divine test that we need not only to know who we are but to know the power of God. Other accounts of Jesus' temptation by Satan are found in Mark 1:12–13 and Luke 4:1–13. The gospel tells us that the Devil departed from Jesus after failing to deceive him. Just like Jesus, we are all on Satan's "most-wanted" list. If Jesus had not known who He was, He too would have been tricked, led astray, and robbed of His true identity.

Another tactic of Satan is to catch us at a weak point, just as he did with Jesus. But we can deal with Satan when he tries to entice us—by knowing who we are in God, staying suited up and prayed up, and knowing the truth!

"Having put on the breastplate of righteousness" (Ephesians 6:14b).

The next time someone asks you if you are in right standing with God, your answer to them should be, "The day I accepted the Lord, He justified me and made me righteous." Righteousness is a gift from God. There is no good deed that you can do to be righteous, because Jesus did it all on the cross. He has done everything required. For, as by one man's disobedience, many were made sinners, so by the obedience of one shall many be made righteous (Romans 5:19).

The "breastplate of righteousness" is a covering for the heart and upper respiratory system. The Greek word used for *righteousness* is *"dikaiosune,"* which is the gracious gift of God given to everyone who believes in Jesus Christ. The gift of being righteous empowers us as believers, making us wiser and stronger than we could have been on our own. The breastplate also covers the lungs to help keep the oxygen flowing. It acts as protection for our souls (hearts) to keep us from being entangled in our own feelings and emotions.

When we put on the breastplate of righteousness, it keeps our heart from becoming vulnerable to the attacks of the Enemy. It says that we believe in Jesus Christ and that He is our Lord and Savior. *Righteousness* is the quality of being holy, pure, and in right standing with God. It means that we stand up for the right thing, even if it is not the popular thing.

"But seek first his kingdom and his righteousness, and all these things will be given to you as well" (Matthew 6:33 NIV).

I believe that one cannot have clear judgment in what is right, unless there exists a clear standard for acting right. That is why the Bible is to be used to govern the lives of Christians. It is full of laws, rules, and guidelines that show us right from wrong. When Lynette's children were small, she purchased some white, leather furniture for her living room and decorated the room with lovely crystal vases. When people came to visit, they were shocked that she had such nice things in her home with three small children running around. I believe that, just as God fashioned the Garden of Eden the way He wanted, Lynette decorated her home the way she liked it—and then laid down the rules to her children.

"And the Lord God commanded the man, saying, 'Of every tree of the garden you may freely eat; but of the tree of the knowledge of good and evil you shall not eat, for in the day that you eat of it you shall surely die'" (Genesis 2:16–17 KJV).

When Adam and Eve made the choice to eat from the forbidden tree, they were not aware of the ripple effect of their disobedience. I know that some of you are thinking that God could have taken the tree and placed it out of the reach of Adam and Eve. He could have moved it to a different location. He could have covered it with plastic, like some of you do with your precious furniture. Instead, God wanted to train His children to obey His rules. If you keep your kids sheltered, they will never learn how to make wise decisions. We all make choices, and depending on what we decide, our consequences will determine the reward or what punishment we will receive.

"For the Lord knoweth the way of the righteous, but the way of the ungodly shall perish" (Psalm 1:6).

God could have forced Adam and Eve to obey Him, but He wanted them to be able to make decisions based on clear standards. One of the attributes of God is that He is righteous. If you want to be declared as the righteousness of God, ask God to impute it to you by faith. Stay right by doing what you know is right.

"And having shod your feet with the preparation of the gospel of peace" (Ephesians 6:15).

We are to have our feet shod with the preparation of the gospel of peace. *Shod* is the term used when describing the act of putting shoes on horses. The horse's hoof is *shod* to protect the hoof or foot and to give traction when running. The foot works together with the body to provide support, balance, and mobility. Putting on the wrong footwear can damage the limb, causing blisters and sore joints throughout the whole body. The right footwear must be worn so that we can run, walk, and go in peace.

The foot and ankle contain twenty-six bones, thirty-three joints, more than a hundred muscles, tendons, and ligaments, and a network of blood vessels, nerves, skin, and soft tissue. A structural flaw or malfunction in any part of the foot can prevent us from readiness. This Scripture puts the emphasis on preparation. *Preparation* is defined as the act of training or groundwork, or putting something together in advance. It is the state of having been made ready beforehand, of readiness or preliminary measure. When a runner enters a race, the first thing he or she does is purchase a good pair of running shoes.

Every believer is assigned to a pulpit. Whether it is at home, at work, at school, or in a grocery line, you are to tell of the good news of Jesus Christ. In Romans 10, Paul talks about how beautiful are the feet of those who preach the gospel of peace, which bring glad tidings of good things. *Peace* means to be free from strife, conflict, chaos, anxiety, and most importantly, sin. When you shod your feet with the preparation of the gospel of peace, you are claiming that the Prince of Peace, Jesus, is victorious over the Prince of Darkness, Satan.

The Greek word used for having your feet shod is *hupodema*, which literally means "to bind together under you." It describes the act of using God's Word as the soles of your shoes so that you are comfortable when you go out into all nations and tell of God's goodness. The preparation of the gospel, like shoes, fits snugly onto you. It means knowing the Word of God and going out with sure steps to tell others about God. Everywhere you walk, whatever place you enter, your feet should be shod with the full knowledge of the gospel so that they will not slip. Once you are prepared, you are to be on your mark, ready, and go swiftly and tell others of the good news of Jesus Christ, which will bring others into His absolute peace.

"The sword of the Spirit, which is the word of God" (Ephesians 6:17b).

Only the Word of God can deal with the soul and reach into the spirit of a man. The Word of God is used as the *sword of the Spirit*. The Greek interpretation of *word* is *"logos,"* but in this passage, the sword of the Spirit refers to *"rhema." Rhema* is having a fresh word from God or biblical Scriptures that can be given instantly. *Rhema* is a revelation, an epiphany that is dropped into you by the Holy Spirit. It is a divine word, fresh off the press from heaven. When the sword of the Spirit is used as a weapon, it annihilates and disintegrates, causing great destruction to the Devil and his kingdom. The Word of God is powerful. Therefore, we must learn how to use the Word of God to defeat the attacks of the Enemy.

"For the word of God is quick, and powerful, and sharper than any two edged sword, piercing even to the dividing asunder of soul and spirit, and of the joints and marrow, and is a discerner of the thoughts and intents of the heart" (Hebrews 4:12).

Studying the Word of God will push you toward becoming a good swordsman. When you properly use the Word of God, it becomes the best piece of weaponry, because it brings defeat to the Devil in battle. The sword does not just represent the entire Bible as one sword but as having the effect of many swords. Every time Jesus was tempted by Satan, He used specific verses to quickly terminate the conversation. For each time Jesus was tempted, He used a different sword or Scripture. He was swift with a response to cut down any attempt by the adversary.

When you memorize Scripture, you become a skilled swordsman. You annihilate, obliterate, and eradicate any lie, trick, or trap that has been set before you, using the Word of God as your sword. It is a trick of the Devil for you to believe that God gave you only one sword to defect many demons. Each Scripture is designed for fighting particular situations. Therefore, each Scripture is relevant, giving you thousands upon thousands of swords to draw from.

Do not get into a debate with Satan without knowing Scripture. Study the Word of God, and be confident in His promises concerning you. If you want to stand, if you want to endure, form your sword by speaking the Word of God. As quickly as the Enemy tosses lies your way, draw the Word of God and smite any doubt or fear. Use your sword to pierce through any attempt or temptation that forms against you, by remembering the promises God spoke in His word concerning the situation you find yourself in.

"Above all, taking the shield of faith with which you will be able to quench all the fiery darts of the wicked one" (Ephesians 6:12). Why does this verse say "above all"? Is the shield of faith more important than the other pieces of armor? Hebrews 11 tells us that without faith it is impossible to please God and that whoever comes to Him must believe that He is a rewarder of them that diligently seek Him. Through faith we understand that the worlds were framed by the Word of God. By faith, Abel offered unto God a more excellent sacrifice than Cain. By faith, Enoch was translated that he should not see death.

How can you try something without having hope or faith that it will work for you? Without the shield of faith, the Devil can tell you all sorts of negative things about God and can plant doubt about the promises God has made concerning you. Without your faith, you can easily be swayed by anything and anyone. In this passage, the *Shield* originally meant "a stone for closing or sealing the entrance to a cave," but later it came to mean "an oblong safegurad," one that covered the soldier during war. God also works as a shield; He protects us from all outside influences and the fiery darts of the Enemy.

The key to this part of the armor is faith. *Faith* is a strong conviction, full assurance of God's revelations and truth. The Greek word for *faith* is "*pisteus*," meaning "the condition of being united or unified." When you unite your faith with the Word of God, you combine or connect your belief in Him to what He has said about you concerning your life. Your trust in God should be like a seal or stamp of approval because of the faith you have in Him through His Son, Jesus Christ. For believers, the whole armor of God should be part of our daily attire, because we are constantly entering into the war zones of life. Satan and his imps are always throwing fiery darts, hoping that you have left yourself uncovered. The only way the Enemy's weapon can penetrate you is if you are not wearing your armor.

Have you been in a conversation where the person said something that you did not take offense to—only to recap later and realize that they tried to harm you with words? The only reason that their little tactic did not hurt you was because you were wearing your armor. People will use words to hit you in the heart, hoping the words will penetrate and stab you like a knife. If you do not guard yourself, others will succeed in doing damage to you that will take years to repair. There were many times when poor Lynette's heart ached from some ungodly emotion that another person caused. If Lynette had known better then, she would have understood that her armor could have shielded her from all those aches and pains the Enemy fired her way.

When you pray to Daddy God to protect your mind and deliver you from all your old patterns of thinking, your loins will begin to produce truth as you walk in the righteousness of God. You will have the peace that surpasses all understanding and the faith that the Word of God will equip you for battle. Never again leave home without your armor, and you will no longer be exposed to Satan's attack. The chart below will give you Scriptures to study as you learn more about your armor.

God's Armor	Know the Truth about...	Affirm Key Scriptures
Belt of Truth	God	Deut. 4:39; Ps. 23:1; 18:1–3
Breastplate of Righteousness	The righteousness of Jesus in you	Ps. 100:3; Rom. 3:23–24; 6:23; Gal. 2:20–21; Phil. 3:8–10
Sandals of Peace	Inner peace and readiness	Rom. 5:1; Eph. 2:14; John 14:27; 16:33; 20:21
Shield of Faith	Living by faith	Rom. 4:18–21; Heb. 11:1; 1 Peter 1:6–7
Helmet of Salvation	Salvation through Christ today and forever	Each day: Ps. 16, 23; Heb. 1:3–6 For eternity: 2 Cor. 4:16–18; 1 Thess. 4:17; 1 John 3:1–3
Sword of the Spirit: God's Word	God's Word countering spiritual deception and accusations	Heb. 4:12; Matt. 4:2–11; 1 Peter 3:15; Ps. 119:110–112

For more information on the *whole armor of God* and a copy of this chart, visit www.crossroad.to/text/articles/armorofgod.html.

There are four positions in this army. Which one are you fulfilling?

- active duty: faithfully serving God
- guard: protecting and serving God's people
- reserve: serve only when called or on special occasions
- AWOL: absent without official leave

"Nay, in all these things they are more than conquerors through him that loved us" (Romans 8:37 KJV).

CHAPTER 7

The Chosen One: Golden Child

And they know that all things work together for good to them
that love God, to them who are called according to his purpose.
—Romans 8:28 KJV

Fathers are not the only ones who have disowned their children. According to *The Washington Times*, the number of single fathers has risen from 600,000 in 1982 to over two million in 2011. This is due to wives and mothers leaving their families. It is said that they leave home for just about the same reasons that husbands and fathers do. They feel that the man can do a better job, they no longer want the responsibility, they feel overwhelmed and cannot take the pressure anymore, or they are just plain selfish ("When Mothers Abandon Their Children or Families," *The Washington Times*). Lynette was not exempt. When her relationship with Anthony's was over, she allowed him to take the kids and go.

In the biological sense, Lynette was an illegitimate parent. Usually the term *illegitimate* is connected with a person who was born to unwed parents. In this case, it means that something was decided incorrectly, that something was not in line with the norm, that the rules had been changed without the input of those involved. This was an unfair act on Lynette's part. It was unacceptable behavior from a living, sober parent, because the children missed out on the love and support of having two parents. If she had known God then the way she knows Him now, she would have known that parenting equals sacrifice of self. Once a person has decided to conceive, they implicitly make a covenant with God that they will cherish, love, and care for that child until young adulthood, because children are a gift from God.

Lynette should have given more hugs, love, and kisses. She should have been there more for their wounds and scars. She hopes her children can forgive her for not being there to place a Band-Aid on their wounds, for not reading bedtime stories or tucking them in at night. She asks for forgiveness that she was not the one who taught them morals and life lessons, that she did not take them to church more often or show them how a real Christian lives. She knows that this book will not bring back the missed years or ease the scars and pains she may have caused them, but she prays that her story will help them and others to move past the pain and insecurities caused by the lack of a mother's love.

This chapter is called "The Chosen One," because there is always that one son or daughter who, regardless of a parent's love and support, will give them the hardest time. When Lynette's youngest son was conceived, she was already raising a three-year-old and a ten-month-old.

Edward was the nice son. He never cried, talked, or made a sound. You would not even know he was around unless he was hungry.

Patrice was quite the opposite. She cried day and night and was always begging. It did not matter what it was; if you had it, she wanted it. (Nothing has changed. She is still begging.)

Lynette's youngest child, Markel, was premature. Lynette did not get the chance to care for him during the first week or so that he spent in the hospital. Lynette also suffered from postpartum depression. Postpartum depression (PPD) is an overwhelming feeling of sadness after the birth of a baby or a major change in the life of a person. While this psychological disorder is not fully understood, some of the contributing factors are poverty, single marital status, prenatal anxiety, childcare, life stress, and low self-esteem, just to name a few.

From an early age, Markel always expressed anger and frustration. At first Lynette was not sure where this was coming from, until she noticed that his behavioral changes always came about after his visits with his father—aka Houdini. This observation is not meant to point out all the errors and problems of Lynette's child. Rather, it is to help parents and teens learn how to work out their issues in a more positive way. Cursing, blaming, name-calling, and striking others are easy to do. Taking control of our own actions is more difficult and challenging, but it is the right and godly thing to do. Knowing why we are angry and directing our anger toward the right person or issue is something we must all learn to do. The Bible tells us that it is okay to get angry, but we are not to sin in the process (Ephesians 4:26, 31).

Anger is provoked or triggered by some perceived threat, conflict, injustice, humiliation, or betrayal. Anger can be destructive or constructive, depending on what our goals and motives are. _Destructive_ anger aims to hurt, humiliate, destroy, and even kill. _Constructive_ anger aims to communicate what triggered the anger and to prevent the recurrence of such hurt and pain. As mentioned in a previous chapter, each one of us suffers from at least one thing that cripples us, like kryptonite did to Superman.

In the case of Lynette's son, his kryptonite happened to be anger. Now, what in the world could an eleven-year-old be so angry about? Could it be the fact that his father was never around? Maybe it was the two jobs Lynette had to work, which prevented Markel from getting the desired attention. Could it be the kids teasing him about his weight? Perhaps it was because of a generational curse that had a strong hold on him. Maybe he just wanted to act out and did not care who got hurt in the process. Was this a sign of drug or alcohol use, or was he acting out of plain old rebellion? His attitude and mentality were so rotten that he was literally destroying his own life and everything around him.

Lynette took her son to see a psychologist at the age of nine. His issues had gotten too much for her, and she felt they needed some professional help. She felt Markel needed someone other than herself to talk with and to share some of his feelings openly. After weeks of sessions with his therapist, things changed slightly. Markel practiced the exercises the doctor showed him, like how to stop and think before responding. This should not have been new to him, because the concepts shown to him by his therapist were things Lynette had already gone over with him. This is not to say that seeking counseling for your child is not helpful. In fact, it is just the opposite.

Child psychologists can help children pinpoint their feelings before an episode occurs. They indirectly help them measure the problems associated with their behavior. In this process, an assessment is developed to see if the child has the skills necessary to modify his behavior. The child learns how to change the way he perceives and responds to events. The counselor observes factors surrounding the child's behavior pattern and assists him in using a positive approach to deal with problems. A hypothesis (tentative explanation) concludes whether to establish a behavior intervention plan.

"Iron sharpeneth iron; so a man sharpeneth the countenance of his friend" (Proverbs 27:17).

It is better to be alone than to be with the wrong company. Friends help shape each others' minds. How we relate and choose our friends is an indication of our interpersonal styles. Interpersonal skills show our behavior and what is likely to influence our interactions with others. If a person has a domineering character, he or she will lead. People with this personality are self-directed, but they can run into a lot of trouble, because they seek the attention of others and will stir up trouble. If a person is shy or passive, he or she can be easily persuaded and will follow rather than lead. On the other hand, people with this kind of personality are not attention seekers, and they are less likely to be viewed as troublemakers.

It is important to pick your friends very carefully. Teens suffer from peer pressure, and when Lynette's son started getting the attention he had longed for, it was, unfortunately, the wrong type of attention. Teenagers are so determined to gain the approval of their peers that they will go to any lengths to receive it. This kind of behavior has caused many of our youth today to operate in rebellion. "For rebellion is as the sin of witchcraft, and stubbornness is as iniquity and idolatry. Because thou hast rejected the word of the LORD, he hath also rejected thee from being king" (1 Samuel 15:23).

What teens fail to realize is that their peers influence them to change their attitudes, behaviors, values, and beliefs in order to fit in. Friends talk friends into behavior similar to their own so that they feel comfortable hanging out together. It is human nature to learn from others, but friends can influence each other to do things that may appear harmless but get them into trouble. Even as I write this, I search for answers as to why our teenagers are so cruel and malicious. Where did this spirit come from? Is it a bloodline curse or what?

Lynette's son walked around with his pants sagging, sporting a do-rag and a cap with the brim turned backward on his head. He somehow thought it was fashionable to wear a stud in one ear, converse with broken language, and act like a brutal, violent thug.

Lynette had begun receiving phone calls from a young man inquiring about a person by the name of AJ. She later learned that they were asking to speak with her son. Her son was not masquerading as a female, was he? He seemed not to be the same little boy that she had given birth to. Many teens, male as well as female, have problems identifying their sexuality. The unisex attire they wear today has become so accepted that it's difficult to determine who is male and who is female. The Bible speaks about such behavior, saying that it is perverted conduct. It is an unclean act and is considered to be an abomination to God, according to Leviticus 18:22. Partakers in this sin dishonor their bodies and are turned over to a reprobate mind (Romans 1:23–28). The phrase "reprobate mind" refers to someone who is confused and cannot distinguish between good and evil, right and wrong.

When our children purpose in their hearts to be defiant, they not only operate in disobedience, but they sin against God. Teens like Markel idolize gangster rappers and others who have negative influence. I am not blaming rap artists for the behavior of our teens, but I dislike a type of music that portrays drugs, sex, and crime in a positive way. I also feel that rappers and those in the public eye should be mindful that kids look up to them and that violence and drugs are not to be glorified.

"Know ye not that the unrighteous shall not inherit the kingdom of God? Be not deceived: neither fornicators, nor idolaters, nor adulterers, nor effeminate, nor abusers of themselves with mankind, nor thieves, nor covetous, nor drunkards, nor revilers, nor extortioners, shall inherit the kingdom of God" (1 Corinthians 6:9–10).

In the fall of 2006, Markel, who had a history of running away, ran away again, and this time Lynette felt some relief. The lies, stealing, and embarrassment had gotten to be a bit much for her. Please do not misunderstand her feelings. She loved her child. She only wished he loved himself. He was old enough to make conscious decisions, but he had chosen to rebel. When Family Services (F.S.), a place for runaway teens, got involved, they told Lynette that she was not liable if Markel decided to leave home. This eased her anxiety somewhat, after all the trouble, heartache, and pain he had caused.

I know that some of you may be appalled at Lynette's attitude and may not understand how a mother could just let her child go. How could she say such cruel and harsh words about her own? As many of these same questions bombarded her own mind, she remembered the story of Moses.

Just as Satan tried to hinder Moses by killing all the Hebrew babies, he goes after each and every one of us. I cannot imagine Moses' mom, Levi, being elated at the idea of putting her son into a basket and watching it sail across the river so he could escape the threats against his life. This event or action does not question whether or not Levi was a good mother, or even if she could take care of her son. It simply shows that she played a great part in the plans God had for Moses by releasing him back to God. It also shows that Satan rages war against godly parents and will stop at nothing to blindside them.

Looking back on the sequence of events before Markel's birth only confirms that there is a calling on his life. Lynette was labeled "high risk" when she was pregnant with him. This was not because she had done anything out-of-the-ordinary or failed to take care of herself. Being placed on "high risk" meant that there was a chance she could lose the baby. That possibility alone elevated her stress level and could have contributed to her postpartum depression.

Two months before Markel was due, Lynette went into premature labor. This was not something that was totally unusual, but it certainly was not the norm for her. The doctor stopped her contractions and placed her on bed rest. Lynette was to remain hospitalized for the next two months to prevent her from having the baby early, but due to complications, they had to induce her labor.

Markel was born two months premature. This little person could be held in the palm of her hand. He was born with undeveloped lungs, which caused him to spend weeks in the hospital. The Devil tried his best to take this baby's life before life had even begun for him. It was a fight for Markel to get into this world, and the fight is still on.

Many of those who are destined for success must travel a road that is not always smooth. Look at Jonah. His refusal to follow God's direction landed him in the belly of a fish. Jonah wanted to do things his own way, and he tried to escape the calling and mandate given to him by God. As we all know, we cannot get away or hide from God. Our desire to do what God wants has to override what we think or want. If it doesn't, we too will be subjected to situations or people who will slow down our development in the things of God.

Too many of our teens are in this same predicament, allowing themselves to be swallowed up by the wiles and cares of this world. Why are so many teens full of anger and rage? Anger has to be triggered by some perceived event. In Markel's case, he generally had no one to blame for the problems in his life. He also learned that punishment is inevitable.

The school year had just started, and he had already managed to earn in-school detention, after-school detention, Saturday detention, and expulsion. So Lynette decided to put him on punishment for the remainder of the school year. He did not think he deserved to be punished and felt that running away from home was better than facing the consequences of his actions. He was not prepared for, nor did he know of, the dangers he would face by leaving the covering of a godly home.

When children are rebellious, their attitude takes them away from the protection of God, which vexes God's spirit. *Vex* means "to irritate, annoy, or afflict." God becomes their enemy, according to Isaiah 63:10. God deals with rebellion faster than any other sin, because we are fighting against His will. When we are out of the will of God, we open ourselves up for more demonic attacks. Lucifer was kicked out of heaven because he turned against God's will.

"And be not conformed to this world: but be ye transformed by the renewing of your mind, that ye may prove what is that good, and acceptable, and perfect, will of God" (Romans 12:2).

In the Bible, Jesus told many stories in the form of parables. The story about the prodigal son in Luke 15 tells of a son who wanted his inheritance so that he could leave his home to wander in the wilderness of the world. Usually a person received his birthright upon the death of a parent. In some cases, a parent gave the child ownership or possession of property and other valuable assets beforehand. This illustration of the prodigal son refers to a lost child, showing how God rejoices when a wayward child repents.

Unlike the son in this parable, Lynette's son did not come to repentance quickly. He stayed out of the home and on the streets, which gave him a false sense of freedom. He was not willing to follow the rules of the house. He felt grown enough to make decisions without guidance, thinking he would find a better way on the streets. He was put into the custody of Family Services (F.S.) and they became his new parents. The moment they got involved, he could no longer return home, even if he had wanted to. He no longer had the love, support, and attention he needed from his family. His needs and desires were not the priority of his new parents, F.S. They were only concerned with placement, which could be a group home or residential home.

Some of you teens think it is cool to call the police on your parents because someone told you that your parent is not allowed to discipline you. Guess what. When the police come to your home, they remove *you* from the home, not the parent. Don't get me wrong. Some teens face serious and dangerous situations where it would be better if they were removed. I am speaking to teens who think they do not have to follow rules and can come and go as they please.

Markel could not have imagined that he would be in that situation for so long. He has been in the F.S. system all his teen life. Every time he has gotten acclimated to his living quarters, he has been uprooted and transferred to another location. He has been in foster care, group homes, and residential homes—all because he wanted to do his own thing. The child Lynette had once fed was now trying to feed her with stuff like, "You were too strict" or "You don't understand." But that was not the problem. The problem was that he felt he was exempt from rules.

This is a call to all teens. I would like to walk you through what you have to look forward to if you decide you no longer want to live under your parents' roof. Once F.S. has taken custody, you are immediately placed in a shelter until they decide placement. A caseworker is assigned, and this person is responsible for getting you into a new school, which can take weeks. They have to find some form of counseling to help you deal with the stress of being alone. You will also spend a great deal of your time going back and forth to court so that the court system can monitor your progress and ensure that you understand what is expected of you.

You are forced to participate in group and individual talk sessions. Refusal to do so only prolongs your counseling, and you are viewed as having depression. They will try to put you on some form of medication, keeping you in a zombie-like state. An assessment is conducted to determine if reunification (going back home) is an option. They poke and pry into your family, because they suspect that this predicament is due to lack of education, drugs, or poverty.

This evaluation can take up to twelve months. The process is so strenuous that you become angry and impatient, and a feeling of hostility overtakes you. You withdraw, causing more attention, which leads to more therapy. Your counselor, who continues to monitor your behavior and attitude, makes recommendations for more counseling and more meds. You spend so much time in therapy and in court that you get behind in school, which can hinder you from graduating on time—unless you attend night school and summer school.

Once your new parent F.S feels the need to keep you in a home setting, they look for a foster home to put you in. This is a temporary placement, and you can bounce from home to home. You could be placed with a biological relative, but if you are known to have behavioral problems, it's more than likely that a family member will not be willing to take on such a challenge.

Once you are placed in a foster home, F.S. monitors your actions and behavior. If your foster parents feel that you are not willing to abide by their rules—which is likely, because it's why you are in this situation in the first place—you are then placed in a group home. A group home is a small, supervised facility, where you have to do daily tasks and are often free to come and go as you please. Once you violate the rules in the group home, you are transferred to a residential home. This placement takes away your freedom to leave the facility, and outside passes have to be earned. In a group home, you are placed at one of four levels.

- At level one, you are on probation for the first two weeks, with no phone calls or outside passes, and you get a weekly allowance of five dollars.
- At level two, you get fifteen minutes of phone privilege, outside passes, a curfew of 8:00 p.m., and a weekly allowance of six dollars.
- At level three, you receive the same conditions as level two, except that your curfew is 9:00 p.m.
- At level four, you get overnight stays with your family, unlimited phone privileges, and a weekly allowance of seven dollars.

Do not even think about running away. Where would you go? Who could you turn to? Think about the friends you've been hanging out with—you know, the ones you lied to your parents to hang out with, the ones who convinced you to change your beliefs, morals, and standards so you could fit in. Where are they now? If you run away, you will become a victim of your own polluted mind. Your only two options are to stay homeless and on-the-run or to return to the shelter you've been placed in. You cannot return home to Mommy, because you have been adopted by your new parents, F.S. In fact, your family will be in trouble if they let you in, because they would be harboring a fugitive.

Wow. Are you sure this is the life you want to live?

The parents' job is to shield their children from the dangers of the world, like the mother hen protects her chicks. She gives out a certain cluck to let her young know that danger is near. This is a call for the young to come under her wings for protection. If you choose to ignore the warning calls and refuse to stay under the wings of protection, you become easy prey. This is true when you rebel against God and His order. Other things in your life begin to change for the worse—even your countenance. When Markel came to visit his family, he did not look the same. His skin was much darker, his hair covered his head like a wild beast, and he had an awful body odor that his mother called a "demonic scent."

Teens, why are you allowing Satan to cause you to lie and manipulate people? His assignment is to steal, kill, and destroy. He does not do this through robbery at gunpoint or drive-bys. He does it by attacking your mind and controlling your thoughts, just as the person behind the steering wheel of an automobile controls the direction of the car. The Devil can control your body if you give him the remote control to your mind.

Satan knows that there is a sensor in the mind that controls the actions of the body. He uses it against you, and that is why the Bible tells us to meditate on the Word of God day and night. Whatsoever things are pure and lovely, think of those things. Occupy your mind with the Word of God, and it will not allow room for the Devil. God commands children to obey their parents. In the Old Testament, rebellious sons were dealt with harshly, usually with immediate death.

"If a man have a stubborn and rebellious son, which will not obey the voice of his father, or the voice of his mother, and that, when they have chastened him, will not hearken unto them: then shall his father and his mother lay hold on him, and bring him out unto the elders of his city, and unto the gate of his place; and they shall say unto the elders of his city, this, our son is stubborn and rebellious, he will not obey our voice; he is a glutton, and a drunkard. And all the men of his city shall stone him with stones that he dies: so shalt thou put evil away from among you; and all Israel shall hear, and fear" (Deuteronomy 21:18–21).

Both the Old and New Testaments promise that if children do not honor their fathers and mothers, their days will be cut off.

"Children, obey your parents in the Lord: for this is right. Honour thy father and mother; which is the first commandment with promise; that it may be well with thee, and thou mayest live long on the earth" (Ephesians 6:1–3).

This Scripture epitomizes the severity of God on young people who disobey their parents. It also tells us that disobedience to parents will cause premature death. Children actually shorten their time on earth when they operate in the sin through disobedience and rebellion. Not only does disobeying your parents show sinfulness of the heart, it's contrary to the Word of God.

Chapter 3 of 1 Timothy talks about how children are to submit to their parents and show them respect. Why do you think God commanded children to obey? My guess would be that parents knows what is best for their children, just as God knows what is best for each of us.

You have been called to accomplish something in life. Just because you are young doesn't mean that God will not use you. Do not continue to let the Devil distract you and influence your thinking, because this can stop the plans God has for you. As with the prodigal son in book of Luke, God is waiting for his sons and daughters to return to Him. You cannot make it without the Father.

God is waiting for His sons and daughters to return home. Come back and be one with your heavenly Father. Do not stay on that road of destruction. If you are operating in rebellion, you are not just fighting against your parents; you are fighting against the will of God. Let God into your life and heart. God wants to restore your lost soul. He is waiting. Will you open up and let Him in today?

Markel has been baptized and now brings souls to Christ.

"I say unto you, that likewise joy shall be in heaven over one sinner that repenteth, more than over ninety and nine just persons, which need no repentance" (Luke 15:7).

CHAPTER 8

Long-Distance Relations: State of Mind

Let this mind be in you, which was also in Christ Jesus.
—Philippians 2:5

Lynette accepted the position that John's friend Ty referred her to. Working at this job was a great experience. She worked in the credit department where they processed credit applications. Months into this position, she was approached by men from all ethnicities, and she grew tired of hearing the same old lines. She was no longer impressed with the money they made, the cars they drove, or the few lines they spoke. If only those men had known the baggage she carried, they would have run like the wind. They were so busy looking at the brick house that they could not see the water damage. If they had looked close enough, they would have noticed the cracks in the bricks and the unstable foundation of her life. If they had paid more attention to her words, they would have heard the mental and emotional state she was in.

Lynette was in a bad state of mind, and she continued to make bad choices. The phrase "state of mind" refers to a person's outlook. In psychology it is referred to as the cognitive process. Cognition is a mental process that includes reasoning, understanding, and decision making. Carl Jung, a psychiatrist of analytical psychology, developed the concept of extroversion and introversion. His theory led to the Myers-Briggs Type

Indicator (MBIT). This quiz is broken into four categories: Extroversion/ Introversion, Sense/Intuition, Thinking/Feeling, and Judging/Perceiving. It was designed to help a person understand his preferences in making choices. If Lynette had been able to understand her strengths and weaknesses, she would have been able to make better choices. For more information or to take the quiz, visit www.humanmetrics.com/cgi-win/ JTypes2.asp.

When people have been emotionally abused and do not take the proper steps to heal, they are in denial. They do not get the help needed to reestablish healthy relationships. Instead, they soak in self-pity and live in unforgiveness. Sweeping feelings under the rug does not make them go away. Lynette's bad attitude was an emotional reaction to the things that had happened to her in the past. She had tried so hard to put the past behind her that she even acted as if her children did not exist. When people do not face and deal with problems, triggers will set them off like bombs, and it's only a manner of time before they explode.

I met a woman who stayed with her husband after he had committed adultery. I thought to myself, *That was mighty courageous of her.* As she spoke about the affair and how this sinful act had almost destroyed her marriage, I could see the hurt and pain she felt. As she continued the conversation, I interrupted and asked, "How long ago did this take place?" She responded with great anger in her voice: "Twenty years ago." Wow. The way she went on and on, I thought it had happened last week. The more I hung around this person, the more I could see that she had never recovered from her husband's betrayal. When she told her story in front of him, I could see in his facial expression, "Here we go again."

The reason that this woman and others like her cannot let the past go, cannot move on, and keep living and rehearsing their hurt is unforgiveness. Forgiveness is not just for other people; it is the key to your breakthrough. I am not saying that she didn't have a right to be angry, but at some point we have to move past the hurt, pain, and disappointments another person has caused us.

"But He was wounded for our transgressions, He was bruised for our iniquities; the chastisement for our peace was upon Him, and by His stripes we are healed. All we like sheep have gone astray; we have turned, every one, to his own way; and the LORD has laid on Him the iniquity of us all" (Isaiah 53:5–6).

If Lynette had given herself the proper time to heal, she would have been in a better position to love and to be loved. Being bombarded by advances daily only placed her in a state of confusion. I felt sorry for the next man in line, because she was going to take him for the emotional roller-coaster ride of his life.

There were, however, benefits from these attention seekers. She received flowers, candy, lunch and gifts from many of them. Out of all these clowns, there was one Hispanic guy who caught her eye. She started noticing this young man, because every time she arrived at work, he somehow met her at the front door and opened it like a perfect gentleman. Lynette had never received that sort of kindness, and she did not know how to handle him. This was new to her, because most fellows would let the door slap her in the face. She had never experienced an interracial relationship, but she felt a desire to interact with him through small talk.

Before long, he and Lynette started taking breaks and lunch together. Jose was a department manager, and she later found out that he had adjusted his work schedule so that the two of them worked the same shift. That arrangement was cool with her, because he started picking her up for work and dropping her off after work.

Many of their coworkers rejected their friendship, which later became a relationship, because interracial relationships were not as popular back then. They were harassed by black men who didn't like the fact that this

Hispanic guy was spending time with a woman who wouldn't give them the time of day. Hispanic ladies could not understand why he would choose a black woman over them. When they went out on dates, people almost always stared at them, whispering and pointing as if they were freaks. Jose ignored the negativity and advised Lynette to do the same, but her attitude was not the greatest, so it didn't take much to set her off. And she *did* go off, with out-of-control behavior.

Anthony was not pleased by the fact that Jose and Lynette were spending time together, so he decided to confront Jose. Jose was not willing to end their relationship. In fact, Anthony's confrontation made Jose even more determined.

Jose was one of the good guys—loyal, honest, and trustworthy. Lynette was in a long-distance relationship with him, not because they lived in two different states but because she was not in a good state of mind. This man cared very much about her, and if she had known then what she knows now, she would have known that you do not mistreat the "good keeps." She was not physically, mentally, or emotionally stable enough to appreciate this good man, because she was not healed or whole. So Jose had only part of her.

Lynette's judgment toward life was so cloudy that she was not living; she was only existing. She was so messed up that she did not recognize the blessing she had. She was living so deep in her past that it was robbing her of a future with a good man and husband. She allowed hurtful situations to block, halt, and hinder any prospect of a successful relationship with anyone, thus returning or, in her case, never leaving a situation that was stunting her growth.

You need to know how to eliminate anyone in your life who stops or hinders you from seeing the blessings of God. If you keep company with the wrong crowd, this can hinder the things God has for you, because you are in the shadow of others and are being hidden and blocked. Lynette should have taken time out to rest from all the labors of life caused by being in wrong relationships. She needed to rest so that she could regain focus with cleared vision to make better decisions. When God commanded Moses to rest on the seventh day, it was to help him hear from heaven and replenish all that he had given out during the week. When we continue to move about without resting, we can't receive the spiritual renewal God intends for us. Spiritual renewal helps us see clearly.

If Lynette had known then what she knows now, she would have known that the adversary plots to keep us in frenzy so we don't take time to regroup and think. Lynette needed to clean house, starting with her mind. The Bible instructs us to renew our minds (Romans 12:2b) and cast down our imaginations and every high thing (2 Corinthians 10:5a). Somewhere along the way, a negative seed had been planted in Lynette's mind. She needed to find it and release it, because it was not serving her well. Because she had allowed harmful words to rent space in her mind, she developed a bad attitude, bitterness, strife, and revenge.

Lynette and her boss did not see eye-to-eye. He was the type who loved to joke and call names. He used a certain tactic to intimidate others by playing a game called "The Dozens." The Dozens is a game of word-sparring or trash-talking. It is a form of trading insults, using demeaning words to humiliate others and thus gain "respect." In today's war of wits, it is known as "snap" or "gunning." Her boss found it easy to insult the ladies in the office. Lynette did not find it funny, nor was it appropriate for him to embarrass these other women in public. She felt that this man needed to be put in his place, but who was going to do it? He had never tried it with her, so she did not want to pick a fight. But who else could have a quick snap at this clown in a way that would shut his mouth for good?

She waited for the opportunity to go toe-to-toe with him, but for some reason he never approached her. She even gave subtle hints to let him know he was out-of-line. She taunted him and poked him, hoping for a bite, but he did not budge. *I know what I can do*, she thought. *I'll wait until he insults another person, and then I can speak up on that person's behalf.* And that was exactly what she did.

One morning while in a meeting, like clockwork, he looked around the room to see who would be his next victim. As he began his attack, Lynette quickly, without hesitation, attacked him. As the entire office burst into laughter, she could tell that this man was humiliated, because his faced turned completely red. He had been an easy target, because he had many flaws. He was a light-skinned brother who wore glasses, had big lips and a high butt, and was pigeon-toed. To top it all off, he was short. Lynette did not let up until she had hit every nerve in his body. He was so furious that he wanted to write her up for insubordination.

Insubordination occurs when an employee willfully disobeys or disregards a superior's instruction or uses abusive language toward supervisors and others. Lynette's boss could not write her up for her actions, because he had initiated this kind of behavior. But the tension that she created for herself caused this man to nitpick, and worst of all, she sacrificed a job promotion.

Weeks after her attack, one of the bosses called her into his office. He told her about a position as manager in the credit department, and he further explained that, because of her attitude, he was going to pass her up and promote a coworker instead. She thought, *You called me in here to tell me that I'm not getting the job?* Before she couldn't get hold of her thoughts, she exploded right in his office. "This is why I didn't give you the job," the boss said.

As she left his office, a sense of embarrassment came over her. She had destroyed any chance for professional advancement. For the first time in her life, she realized that her words not only pierced the hearts of others but weakened her as well. She was ashamed at the way she had carried herself for so many years. If she had known God then as she knows Him now, she would have known not to be conformed to this world. She should not have allowed herself to be enticed into exchanging insults with that person—or anyone else, for that matter. She should have known that life and death are in the power of the tongue. According to the book of James, she was executing others with her tongue.

"And the tongue is a fire, a world of iniquity: so is the tongue among our members, that it defileth the whole body, and setteth on fire the course of nature; and it is set on fire of hell" (James 3:6).

She should not have gotten pleasure and accolades by administrating hurt, pain, and shame on another. She should have known that this was not the way a child of God behaved. We should all realize that there are consequences of such behavior. Having the wrong attitude produces wrong ideas, bad patterns of thinking, manipulation, and self-indulgence.

Consider what Lynette sacrificed for jumping into a fight that was not her own. Who was she to step in and try to save the drowning, when she herself was sinking? Was she acting like a god? She was in a position to promote peace, but instead she started war. She should have been celebrating life, but she was so busy cutting people up with her tongue that she created death.

Lord, please forgive us for using our unruly tongues to plant seeds of bitterness in others.

"Therefore if any man be in Christ, he is a new creature: old things are passed away; behold, all things are become new" (2 Corinthians 5:17).

I've heard the expression that "attitude is everything." What people fail to realize is that a bad attitude can _block_ everything. Where do our attitudes come from? We can blame our upbringing, circumstances, or situations. The fact is that our attitudes come from within. For twenty-four years of Lynette's life, she had been wrestling with a bad attitude that she should have received a BA degree (Bad Attitude Degree). Having the wrong attitude can hinder our walk with God. It can block and halt us spiritually, intellectually, emotionally, and—as you can see from Lynette's experience—financially.

Our attitudes and actions determine whether we succeed or fail. A positive attitude leads to success, and a negative attitude leads to failure.

Success	Failure
desire and drive	procrastination
determination	lack of will power
commitment	lack of resolution
discipline	fear of the unknown and of success
courage	poor self-control
perseverance	complacency
optimism	pessimism
abundance	scarcity
self-esteem	low self-esteem
knowledge	ignorance
experience	naïveté
organization	disorganization

"That ye put off concerning the former conversation the old man, which is corrupt according to the deceitful lusts; and be renewed in the spirit of your mind" (Ephesians 4:22–23).

It's no wonder that Lynette and others like her fail in their personal lives—and for the same reason that many of us cannot get ahead. Our failure to succeed and grow as individuals is often the result of many negative characteristics. As Lynette struggled to clean up her act, her manager started to notice a change in her. In fact, he tested the waters to see if it was just a facade. He began to rag on her, which is another form of trash-talking, but she did not say a word. The other ladies in the office were so disappointed that she lost "cool" points with them. As she began to practice self-control, she realized that people like her manager needed to put others down just to make themselves look better and bigger. A blessing came out of her transformation: she was promoted to manager.

Jose and Lynette were now both managing, giving them the flexibility to operate and schedule things the way they wanted. They took the same days off and scheduled vacation times together. They acted like no one else existed. Anthony felt pressured. He felt that he had to do something and do it quick, so he decided to propose.

Lynette was so excited about the ring that she didn't even think to give Anthony an answer. She wore her ring, showing it off to her family and friends without even thinking about Jose's feelings. Since they worked so closely together, everyone assumed that the two of them were engaged. She tried to convince Jose that the ring didn't mean a thing and that it was just a gift. What was a girl to do?

Jose demanded that she take the ring off, and Anthony insisted that she keep it on. Jose was so determined to win that he went out and bought her another ring. She was more confused than ever—to the point that she sometimes wore Anthony's ring when she was with Jose and Jose's ring when she was with Anthony. She decided to wear both rings, just to keep peace of mind for herself, and that was exactly what she did.

One morning as she attempted to get dressed for work, she felt nauseated. It seemed as if she regurgitated everything she had eaten for the entire week. Her body did not change, and she didn't miss her cycle, so she knew it was not related to pregnancy. But what else could it be?

As the weeks went by, she decided to visit her doctor. The pregnancy test came back negative. She noticed Jose eating more, gaining weight, and sleeping like he was on drugs. Although her test had come back negative, Lynette was sure she was pregnant. The only problem was that she had to tell Anthony that he was not the father.

Jose was all gung ho about becoming a dad, and he treated her even better than he had before. Lynette felt that she was reaping the harvest of her sinful act. How could she feel good about being out of the will of God? Reaping a harvest meant that a seed had been planted, and the only seed growing in this garden was a baby. She had lost so much weight that people couldn't even tell she was pregnant. Anthony's feelings for her had not changed, and he even told others that they were having a baby, even though he was not the father.

Jose could not understand why Anthony was just as excited for this baby as he was. Lynette had to persuade Jose that he was the father and that Anthony was just doing this as a scare tactic. In the end, Jose could no longer deal with all her baggage and drama. He decided to join the military to get away. Was she so bad that this man would rather go to war than fight for her love? Had this man been in her private boot camp for so long that he was willing to strap a bomb to himself just to escape his duties as her personal baggage handler? Was she using her situation with Anthony as a crutch to the point that she had become emotionally and physically crippled?

"A double minded man is unstable in all his ways" (James 1:8).

This was a wake-up call. The state she was in became crystal clear to her. She was in a world of "so what," "I don't care," and "whatever." She walked around like all was well, like she had it going on. She had been caught in a twister and was in a place called Oz, an unknown place in her mind that she could not see, and clicking her heels would not bring her back to a state of peace. She needed something or someone to help her escape her confusion. In her sad condition, she insanely kept doing the same things, expecting different results. In the end, her state of uncertainty had hurt only herself. Living with a man she no longer loved, she had lost out on the possibility of happiness with a man who was good to her—even as she piled more garbage in her bags with another pregnancy.

Lynette cried as loudly as she could, "Lord, I need help!" She was in a long-distance relationship with herself, others, and God because of sin. If you are in a state of perplexity because of your choices, there's no time like the present to invite God into your heart and mind. God is willing and able to deliver you from the agonies of your condition, but you have to be open, honest, and willing to allow Him access. Take your cares and burdens to God, and leave them there, because God cares and will deliver you now! Stay focused on God, and let Him lead you.

Deliverance is nigh to thee, even in thy mouth. "But what saith it? The word is nigh thee, even in thy mouth, and in thy heart: that is, the word of faith, which they preach" (Romans 10:8 KJV).

CHAPTER 9

The Nutcracker: Woops upside the Head

An angry man stirreth up strife, and a furious
man aboundeth in transgression.
—Proverbs 29:22

Lynette had always heard about "The Nutcracker," and for some reason she'd thought it was a Christmas story, because December was the only time of year she heard others talking about it. After researching it, she learned that "The Nutcracker" was a folktale, and it reminded her of the tale of "The Sleeping Beauty." "The Nutcracker" was a story about a girl named Clara who fell asleep and dreamed that she had been given a nutcracker prince. Legend said that a nutcracker represented power and strength and that it served as a trusty watchdog that guarded a family from danger and evil spirits. The nutcracker was a toy soldier with an awful, grim look about him.

Lynette would have loved to have a captivating prince in her life to protect her. But her fighting soldier had a defect: instead of protecting her, he attacked her. Had she misunderstood what a nutcracker was, or had her way of life cause her "nutcracker" to go woops upside her head? Unlike Clara's dream, Lynette's life had become a living nightmare.

The day was nothing special when she met Walter. As a matter of fact, she was already five months pregnant with her third child. It was the summertime, and like clockwork, the kids had gone to spend time with their grandfather for the entire summer. Anthony and Lynette were still living together; she was still in a long-distance relationship with Jose, because in was in the service; and she didn't have any room for another person in her life—or so she thought.

While hanging out with her friend Ann, Lynette learned that Ann knew someone who wanted to meet her. Ann explained that this man knew of her situation and still wanted to talk with her. Given her current condition, Lynette wasn't comfortable with the idea of meeting him.

One day Lynette and Ann decided to visit Ann's grandmother. As the car pulled up to Madea's house, there stood a dusty, well-built young man on the porch. As he approached the car, Ann quickly informed Lynette that this was the man who had wanted to meet her. As he drew closer, Lynette could not see much of his face because she was so fixated on his legs.

They engaged in small talk, and Walter invited her in to see his masterpiece. He was a self-employed carpenter, electrician, and plumber. You name it, he did it. She was impressed with what this brother could do with his hands. They exchanged phone numbers, and he gave her a special code that he would use if Anthony happened to answer the phone.

Was this a warning sign of Walter's cunning ways, or was this brother teaching Lynette something that would be useful for future endeavors? Was this enchanting prince looking out for her best interests? Should she be concerned about the situation, or was she making too much out of it?

Anthony did not spend much time at home, and Jose was still away in basic training, so Lynette guessed that she had time for a little fun after all. She and Walter spent every waking moment together. She went over to his house for breakfast, and they dined together for lunch and dinner.

They had grown so close so quickly that they almost didn't have time for work. As the end of the summer drew near, Lynette was a little nervous, because things would surely change once the kids returned home.

Walter assured her that her kids would not be a problem. In fact, Walter lived with his sister, and there were plenty of kids around, so her kids would fit right in. Walter was close to his family, and they welcomed her kids. They even watched the kids so that Walter and Lynette could spend time together. Things couldn't get any better, right?

Once the baby was born, Jose returned home. Walter and Lynette had begun to create a bond, while Anthony and Lynette had remained roommates. She thought this was great, but as each man demanded more of her, she was spreading herself so thin that it started to get complicated. Anthony confronted Jose; Jose and Walter bumped heads; and Walter and Anthony fought. The three male figures in her life were so irate with each other that everything in her life was turning out all wrong.

How could a situation that seemed to work so well for her turn out so nuts for everyone else? How could they not understand the situation they had all agreed to? Anthony knew the baby wasn't his; Jose knew she was still living with Anthony; and Walter knew she was pregnant with Jose's child. So what seemed to be the problem?

She pulled herself out of the equation and waited patiently to see who would be the last man standing. Anthony decided that he could no longer handle the complexities of their so-called relationship, so he decided to take their two kids and move out. Jose felt that as long as he could spend time with his son, he too would step out of the picture. Walter wanted to stay and form a union with her already-made family, and so their lives began.

They decided to keep the apartment that Anthony and Lynette had shared, so they wouldn't have to go apartment hunting. Three years into this fairy-tale relationship, all seemed well. For the first time in ten years, Lynette decided to make a commitment to a monogamous relationship.

Yes, men tried to get with her, and yes, she was tempted, but her desire to commit to only one man was greater than the game she had mastered for many years. She and Walter appeared to be a perfect couple, so in sync that people complimented them on what a loving and supportive relationship they had.

Walter knew so much about her and was so attentive that she had no room to even look at another man, even if she'd wanted to. He became her best and only friend. He became so close to her that he left no room for anyone else. He knew things about her that she had not even told him. He knew where she was at all times and how long it took her to go from point A to point B. He was better than a GPS, knowing how many miles it took her to travel and even keeping a good watch on the mileage so she wouldn't go over the allotted distance. He knew what she wore, both her inner- and outerwear. This man knew everything about everything. Was that amazing or what?

He had addresses and phone numbers for every person she came in contact with. When she was not at a designated place, he would call around to find her location. She thought nothing of it at first. She thought that she *should* let her man know where she was and how long she was going to be gone. Lynette thought it showed respect on her part to inform her man of all her whereabouts.

The day that she returned home from an unscheduled trip to the mall was the end of a good thing and the beginning of a "nutcracker." Lynette's ending was not as enchanting as Clara's, as her nutcracker did not turn into a handsome prince. Her fairy-tale relationship with Walter turned into a living nightmare. If she had known God then, she would have known that mind games are meant to direct and influence the pattern of a person's behavior. She should have known that allowing Walter to isolate and separate her from her family and friends was an attempt to control and manipulate her.

I wish I could have warned Lynette that the Enemy was trying to set her up to kill and destroy her. She did not know that this was only the beginning of what could turn out to be a tragic end to her life. The tables turned so quickly in this relationship that Lynette couldn't recall when Walter turned into a boxer—and she turned into his punching bag.

All she knew was that he fought her like he was the heavyweight champion of the world. The more information this man knew about her, the more abusive he became, and each day that they were together, they fought. If he came in after having a bad workday, they fought. If she wore a certain outfit, they fought. If a man looked at her in a certain way, they fought. If someone complimented her, or if she smiled, laughed, cried, or coughed, they fought. They fought about everything. The worst part was that the more she fought back, the worse she got beaten.

When they realized that she was pregnant, Walter vowed that he would never put his hands on her again. If only she could have known the number of times an abuser tells his victim that lie. She would have known that after a man hits a woman for the first time, he will do it again, nine times out of ten.

Walter got a part-time job, so he was gone both day and evenings. His work schedule guaranteed that he would not be around enough to fight Lynette. Right. She took a snapshot of her situation and knew that something was missing, but she didn't know what. She had never felt so alone. She had to find something that could lift her out of this pit she had dug for herself. Walter was so controlling that Lynette had allowed him to separate her from all her family and friends. She was afraid to let anyone know what she was going through, because she could not take their criticism.

Women like Lynette are not strong enough to hear someone say, "Just leave." They are not emotionally strong enough to hear someone say, "Why are you letting him do this to you?" When a woman is in this type of situation, she can't see herself doing any better. When she loves someone, regardless of how much danger she is in, she tries to convince herself that there's hope or that the person will change and will no longer inflict pain on her.

As she began to pray and seek God's face, Lynette knew right then that she had neglected her spiritual life for so long that she was being eaten alive in her world of sin. If only she had known that God is faithful and just and that He would forgive her of her sins and cleanse her from all of her unrighteousness. If only she had known to confess her sins and turn away from them!

In the beginning of their relationship, Walter had showed Lynette signs of his abusive ways, but she had ignored them. Many women are so afraid to be alone that they would rather look past the negative, poisonous behavior and instead try to nurture it and fit in with it. They somehow think that this is a form of love. They feel a false sense of security that masquerades as love, so they stay, hoping things will get better, thinking that they can change him. But a woman can't change a man!

"Let no man say when he is tempted, I am tempted of God: for God cannot be tempted with evil, neither tempteth he any man: but every man is tempted, when he is drawn away of his own lust, and enticed" (James 1:13–14).

Lynette felt that God was punishing her for all the wrong she had done and that she deserved everything she got. There are things that God allows into our lives to help our faith grow, and there are things that happen because we operate in disobedience and sin. Sin separates us from the love and protection on God. Lynette was in this place because she had been drawn there by her own lust and desires. Lynette's problem was that she had never totally surrendered to the Lord. God does not cause bad things to happen to us, but He has promised that He will let all things work together for our good (Romans 8:28).

Walter worked extremely hard to get his life together. He stopped selling drugs, stopped drinking, and found himself a job working nights. Lynette was happy with this arrangement, because it gave her the opportunity to do things she had always wanted to do, things she'd never had the time or money to do. Once Walter had recommitted himself to his kids, she was able to shop more and buy herself things she wanted to have. She shopped so much that she started neglecting her responsibilities at home. The only time she paid the monthly bills was when she received a disconnection notice. Lynette had been neglected for so long that she overcompensated with overspending.

When a woman is in a violent relationship, there is a cycle of behavior. At this point, Lynette and Walter were in the reconciliation stage. This is the stage where the abuser apologizes for his actions and makes it up to the woman by buying candy and roses. He is forgiven, and the couple enters the calm of the honeymoon phase—until something happens to cause his tension to build, and another incident occurs. Lynette was blindsided when she forgot about all the rage that was trapped in the man she had once loved. It was not until the night that Walter came home from a party that she realized she had to choose between life and death.

Violence against women happens every day. There are numerous cases where a woman maliciously attacks a man, but the number of attacks against women and children are so overwhelming that abuses on men are overlooked. The three Goliaths that Lynette had to deal with in this relationship were sex, violence, and alcohol. "Goliath" is a metaphor that describes someone who is bigger or stronger than another person and who throws his weight around. "Goliaths" take an overbearing position to intimidate others. Because they are tortured by their own demons, they will wreak havoc in the lives of others.

Most abusers use drugs or alcohol as an excuse for their violent acts, but they are no more than cowards. Abusers blame others for their behavior. They try to justify themselves, spouting reasons that they have been forced into their violent temper and unchecked anger. Anger equals hatred, which leads to rage, and before long, victims find themselves in violent situations.

If you are with someone who operates in jealousy, rudeness, insults, and intimidation, violence will follow. If you are in a relationship that is controlling, and your partner blames you for everything, it's likely that you are in danger of an abusive attack. I know that some of you who are in abusive relationships would say, "He has never put his hands on me," but a verbal attack can cause more damage than a physical altercation. If your mate has to punch holes in the wall to calm down, more likely than not he has anger problems. If your mate throws things across the room, yells, cusses, and screams, you could wind up in a faceoff with an overly aggressive abuser.

One night after Lynette had fallen asleep on the couch, she woke up to find Walter standing over her with a knife. As her screams echoed, she realized that she had to do something. If she could not leave Walter for her own safety, she had an obligation to do it for her kids. She called the police and had him arrested for assault. She packed enough clothes for a week, changed the locks on the door, and stayed with her girlfriend for a week.

Walter searched high and low, trying to find her, and when he finally spotted her car, he began stalking her like a bloodhound. He left all kinds of threatening messages at her job, with friends, and on cell phones. He contacted her by every means, threatening to kill her mother, the kids, and anyone else whose loss would bring grief upon her. She was able to use these contacts as evidence to get a restraining order against him. Then she would be able to live a safer and happier life. Right.

Once the restraining order was put in place, Walter's anger—and stalking—only intensified. This devil of a man wasn't going to let Lynette just walk out on him. He made sure that her road to freedom would be a hard one. There were many obstacles standing in the way of her being delivered and set free. Every move she made toward freedom made Walter more determined to get her back. He was like a bulldozer, and anyone or anything that stood in his way was going to get crushed. He stalked and called and called and stalked. There was no end to this "nutcracker." This man made stalking a full-time job, and Lynette did not feel safe. Her life was no longer her own. He controlled her life through fear, and because she feared the unknown, she had to be in the house by a certain time each day.

Stalking is a legal term for repeated harassment or other forms of invasion of a person's privacy in a manner that causes fear to its target. Being stalked is a life-changing process. Stalking victims are in a state of constant fear, twenty-four hours a day. The ongoing nature of stalking can cause traumatic psychological damage to the victim. Statistics show that one million people in the United States have been stalked. The majority of stalking victims are ordinary people, mostly women, who are being pursued and threatened by someone with whom they have had a prior relationship. Approximately 80 percent of stalking cases involve women stalked by ex-boyfriends and former husbands. The National Center for Victims of Crime has additional information on federal and state laws at its website: www.ncvc.org/law/Stalking/stalking_frames.htm.

Common categories of violence against women include: domestic violence, spousal abuse, partner abuse, woman-battering, dating violence, sexual assault, date rape, marital rape, acquaintance rape, rape by a stranger, and homicide. If you are in violent relationships, find some way—other than death—to get out. Don't let another day go by without praying to God to give you the strength and courage to leave. Domestic violence is abuse that happens to an individual through a spouse, a former spouse, a fiancé, a boyfriend or girlfriend, or a cohabitant.

It is estimated that an act of domestic violence occurs every fifteen seconds somewhere in the United States. That figure translates to over 2.5 million victims per year. This abuse affects the lives of the victim and the children who live within the boundaries of these abusive relationships. If you don't want to save your own life, at least save the life of that child. Get help today.

"If my people, which are called by my name, shall humble themselves, and pray, and seek my face, and turn from their wicked ways; then will I hear from heaven, and will forgive their sin, and will heal their land" (2 Chronicles 7:14).

Lynette found a church and began to put the pieces of her life back together. She attended Sunday school and Bible class, and she was there every time the doors of the church were open. She fasted and prayed, connecting back to the only person who could help her in that desperate time.

Stop right now and thank God for always giving us another chance.

I pray that God will take away the hurt you suffer from the negative things that inadequate people have brought upon you. I pray that the memories of ungodly relationships, distorted environments, and encounters that have caused disastrous scars will be removed and no longer effect you. May the spirit of unforgiveness be loosed from you, even as the power of the spirit of forgiveness is forever bound to you. I pray that God will mend your heart and that you will continually be made perfect for the ministry within you from God. I pray in the name of our Lord and Savior, Jesus Christ, that you will be totally healed and delivered. Amen!

"Heal me, O LORD, and I shall be healed; save me, and I shall be saved: for thou art my praise" (Jeremiah 17:14).

CHAPTER 10

Owe No Man: Entrapment

Owe no one anything, except to love one another; for
he who loves his neighbor has fulfilled the law.
—Romans 13:8

I owe, I owe; it's off to work I go. How many of you can relate to this
frame of reference? It seems like you work only to pay bills. You live from
paycheck to paycheck. In fact, some people may feel that they are just one
check away from being bankrupt.

Lynette's problem wasn't that God did not make good on His promise
that the "blessing maketh rich and adds no sorrow" (Proverbs 10:22). The
problem was that she was not a good steward of her finances.

Lynette received her first credit card in her early twenties. The thought
of purchasing now and paying later was like a dream come true for her.
Before long, she had all of her favorite department store charge cards
and even three major ones. She thought it was nothing to pay off a new
suit next month for what she had purchased today. She was the "cat's
meow," or so she thought. She was all dressed in the finest of linen, and
her pockets were lined—but there was no money in them. She was the
envy of all who knew her, but when those bills started rolling in, this life
of purchasing on credit threw her.

She claimed that she was not about to use her whole paycheck to pay off something she no longer owned. She said that these companies must have lost their minds to think that she was about to pay them 21 percent finance charges on $1,800 monthly bill. The finance charge on her first month's bill was $109.40. Now, Lynette's mathematical skills were not the greatest, but when she received her first statement, she was shocked to discover her mathematical findings.

Lynette had a credit line of $2,500.00 on a revolving charge card with 21% finance charges (APR). She had charged $1,800.00 before she received her first bill.

$1,800.00 x .21 =	$378.00
Balance:	$2,178.00 (with finances charges)
First payment:	$109.40 (part amount toward principle)
Balance:	$2,069.00 x .21 = $413.80 (finances charges)
Second payment	$2,503.49 x .21 = $525.73 (finances charges)
Third payment	$3,029.22 – $109.40 x .21 (minimum payment)
New balance	$3,532.98

"*I owe what?*" she yelled.

What Lynette had failed to realize was that those shrewd monsters had only applied a small amount of her payment toward the principle of $1,800.00. Most of the payment went toward the finance charges. The worst part of this whole learning process was that she had not factored in her monthly necessities. And this amount of debt was for only one credit card; she had more to tally up. At that rate, it could take thirty or more years to pay off that one credit card.

They got me twisted, she thought. *They shouldn't have trusted me. They should have known that young people are irresponsible. I don't care about some credit report. I don't even know what that's about anyway. What do I care about buying a house right now? I still live with my momma. I don't care what they say. Mr.*

Collection Man can threaten me all he wants. I'm not listening! Lynette had a terrible attitude toward her financial obligations and was unaware that her actions were a snapshot of her character.

When people are locked financially, they can't do anything without the possibility of selling themselves short and compromising their worth. Lynette was not free; she was enslaved by those giant intuitions we call collection agencies.

Caller: "Hello."

Lynette: "Hello."

Caller: "Can I speak to Lynette?"

Lynette: "She's not here. Would you like to leave a message?"

Caller: "To whom am I speaking?"

Lynette: "I'm sorry, she's not here. Would you like to leave a message?"

Caller: "Can you tell her that this has been our third attempt to collect on an outstanding debt and we need to hear from her? When is the best time to call back?"

Lynette: "I'm not sure."

Caller: "Please make sure she gets this message."

Lynette: "No problem." Click.

Does this sound familiar? There's nothing like answering your phone and disguising your voice from the person on the other end. You may say to yourself, "Thank God for caller ID." No, ask God for wisdom so that you can be a good steward over your finances. Our society has made it so that you must have some credit established in order to purchase a major item such as a car or house. Young people who have just finished college, or people who pay by cash, may find this to be disheartening and disappointing.

In order to get a loan, a person has to have accrued some form of debt already, and bad credit is better than no credit. This sounds like a setup, a trap, a scheme, and a recipe for failure. According to the Federal Reserve Board, consumer debt has hit $1.98 trillion. This figure represents credit card debt and car loan debt but excludes mortgages. The American Bankers Association recently reported that credit card delinquencies, or missed payments, has reached a milestone of 4.09 percent, and it predicts that the delinquency will rise to 4.34 percent from 4.08. According to the American Bankruptcy Institute (ABI), personal bankruptcy filings have nearly doubled in the past decade, rising 7.4 percent to more than 1.6 million.

What does the Bible say about debt? Romans 13:7–10 says, "Owe nothing to anyone except to love one another." In the context of paying taxes and keeping the Ten Commandments, Paul commanded the believer in the strongest possible terms to literally "owe no man anything, nothing at all." When you pay all you owe (monthly necessities), then and only then are you free to fulfill your debt of love toward one another.

Friends, it can be shown time and time again that when a Christian becomes indebted for reasons other than true poverty, it is generally because he or she is not a good steward over that which God has entrusted to them. Spending beyond your means becomes obvious when you must work overtime or take a second job in order to pay your debts. When you are working that hard to make ends meet, your children are being robbed of your presence—and the love and affection they need from you. I'm not saying that having credit cards is all bad. Just understand that if you can't handle the responsibility of paying off your debts, don't incur them.

Please hear me, all you college students. You will have enough financial obligation when you're paying back school loans. Don't allow yourselves to get caught up in credit card debt as well. We must educate our young people to the fact that those greedy loan institutions will hunt them down in an attempt to entrap them in debt. Don't allow the opportunity to "buy it today, pay it tomorrow" to entice you into falling for these cunning and deceptive plots. The truth is, you will be paying for what you no longer possess for over three decades. If you can't pay off your purchase in full when the bill comes, the interest rates alone, not to mention late fees, will rob you.

If only Lynette had known this, I'm sure she would not have gotten so deep in credit card debt. She did not know what a credit report was or who Equifax, Experian, and Transunion were. She later found out that these were the three major "credit bureaus" that financial intuitions report to regarding your payment history. They keep a track record of all your transactions involving revolving accounts and loans. They help other creditors decide whether to trust you with further loans or credit. It has gotten to the point that utility companies and landlords now report your payment history to them as well.

There is a statute of limitations for delinquent debt. In the state of Illinois, all written contracts and promissory notes will stay on your credit report for up to seven years, and in some cases, ten years. Lynette said, "If only I had known then what I know now, I would have acted more responsibly and maturely in repaying a debt or loan." Having credit demonstrates your personal character, and if it is handled improperly, it hinders future purchases such as a car or home.

Beware of companies that promise to clean up your credit report for a low fee. The law on delinquencies is designed to follow you for up to ten years, so how can a company make claims that they can have these problems removed? This is just another way the Devil sifts your finances. The process is to find a loophole in the way and reason that companies report to credit bureaus. Yes, creditors who did not follow proper protocol are challenged, but once they have properly documented your default, the item in question is put back on your credit report.

It wasn't until Lynette wanted to purchase a car that she realized that her reckless behavior from ten years earlier still showed up on a credit report. It was attached to her social security number, her last known address, and her date of birth. She now realizes that she had the wrong attitude about her financial responsibility and obligations.

Depression became common, because her finances were so low that she couldn't even afford to pay her monthly bills. She had been in church all her life and had paid her tithes, so she couldn't understand why she was so short on money. She began to pray and ask, "Why, Lord? You told me that if I paid my ten-percent tithes, you would rebuke the Devil for my sake." She questioned God, because she wanted to know what had gone wrong. *Why am I struggling to make ends meet?* she wondered. Truth be told, her ends were so far apart that they *never* met. She was bound up, messed up, and tied up in her finances. She cried out to God, because she needed to know what she could do to see above her situation.

God gave her the harsh reality that if she wanted to become debt-free, she had to get an extra part-time job. *Now, Lord,* she thought, *I don't even want to work a full-time job, so you know I will not do well working a second job. Besides, I don't have the time or energy to work part-time, and if I have to work, I'm not going to take a job where I can't make a certain dollar amount.*

As you know, if God is in a plan, He will make things fit together. Not only was Lynette making more money than she'd wanted, but she did not have to travel—because she worked part-time within the same company but in a different department. God showed her how to get out of debt in less than a year. Lynette was debt-free, and she is no longer prey to those bully collection agencies.

Lynette's story may not work for everyone, but I would like to share the strategy that God gave her, hoping it helps someone else. First, she had to admit that she had a spending problem and that she wanted to be set free of it. She then tallied up all her bills so she knew how much she owed. She decided to work a part-time job for the sole purpose of getting out of debt. That way she was not taking funds from the household income to pay off the credit card mess she had created. She then decided which debt to pay off first. She also called each credit card company to have them close the account.

The reason for this action was to prevent her from having the store call the credit department to get her account number so that she could make a purchase using the account. Focusing on one card at a time, she made payments every two weeks until she was at a zero balance. She repeated this process until all her credit card debts were paid, and she was no longer trapped and bound by her finances. Many financial professionals say that closing accounts negatively affects your credit score, but if you are already in trouble, this process will help you get out of trouble and will give you a fresh start to reestablish yourself.

Lynette thanked God for helping her regain control over her finances, but that was just the first stage of total freedom.

"If any of you need wisdom, ask God for it. He will give it to you. God gives freely to everyone. He doesn't find fault" (James 1:5 NIV).

Lynette loved coupons and hated to shop without them. One day as Lynette separated her mail, she was distracted by all the coupons and catalogs she had received. As her thoughts raced and the expectation of using these coupons increased, God began to minister to her and showed her that coupons were just another tactic to get people to spend money. God had revealed to her that coupons were a way that business owners got people to think only about the saving aspect of the deal, while their intent was to get people in to their establishments to spend.

She received coupons from her favorite restaurants. One of them advertised that she could save ten dollars on her next purchase. The intent was not only to get her in but also to entice her in within a certain time frame by using expiration dates. The expiration dates told her that she had a certain amount of time to cash in on these "great deals."

Let's break down the strategy by using basic economics. Lynette had not intended to visit, because she was trying to save money by not eating out. She received a ten-dollars-off coupon in the mail. She knew it would take at least fifty dollars to feed her family. She went to the restaurant so she could save ten dollars by spending fifty dollars or more. The coupon also required that she dine in to cash in on this great deal. This was to lure her into ordering more, as people tend to spend less on takeout than they do when they dine in. Tell me, who wins here?

Lynette was a coupon queen and hated to shop without them, but she felt the need to expose the tricks and plots behind the things that were meant for good. Satan is the master of trickery, and he is good at twisting things around to cause us to stumble. If you are already planning on shopping, I strongly advise you to keep the coupons in your purse or car so that you can take advantage of the savings. You can also search the web and newspapers for store coupons. But don't shop just to use the coupons, because you are not saving money. That is the trick.

Satan strikes again! December is such a great time. It's the time of year when people have the spirit of giving. We all know that the most important time of the year is the birth of our Lord and Savior, Jesus Christ. Christmas should be a time of love, thanksgiving, and sharing. Christmas should be a time when family and friends come together for precious moments of celebrating Christ and exchanging gifts. Unfortunately for many families, Christmas has become a time of depression and loneliness. What has happened to the spirit of the season? Have people become so commercialized that they allow Satan to steal their joy, even during a time of thanks and praise to God for His life with us here on earth?

Stop getting trapped or feeling pressured into buying until all of your credit cards are maxed to their limits. It should not hurt to give. Giving is one of the spiritual gifts God has given to us. It should not take you a whole year to pay off gifts you purchased for Christmas. Again, we need to keep our spiritual antennae up so that we can see Satan's attack from afar. We need to be more spiritually connected so that his attacks will not hit our finances like a tsunami.

"Do not be anxious about anything, but in everything, by prayer and petition, with thanksgiving, present your requests to God" (Philippians 4:6 NIV).

When Lynette found herself anxious to go shopping or to make a decision about spending, she almost always wished she had waited. We live in a society where everything is express, instant, quick, fast, and in-a-hurry. The Bible warns us about being careful and says not to worry about anything.

During the income tax season, many of us consider taking a "refund anticipation loan" or the next-day or three-day refund. We overlook the fact that this process costs us hundreds of dollars. This so-called rapid refund takes advantage of those of us who, like Lynette, are anxious to get our money faster. This is money that we have not only worked hard for but have waited a whole year to get back. If only we would wait an extra week, we could get our refunds within a couple of weeks and avoid the extra charges.

We fail to recognize that we are just taking out a high-interest loan on money we have already earned. This scheme is targeted mostly to low-income families and is another way to keep us in that "poor" mentality. We can get our entire refund (minus processing fees) if we are not anxious and just wait that extra week or two. Once Lynette was able to apply Philippians 4:6 to her life, she was no longer enticed by catchphrases like *rapid*, *instant*, and *express* associated with advertisements, because she knew there was a costly price tag.

What about the trend seekers? They have to wear the latest fashions and will pay anything to do so. Lynette too was a "designer" queen. Everything in her closet had to have a brand-name label. One day while she was out shopping, the Holy Spirit educated her on the true meaning of bargain shopping.

Lynette was on her way to a particular store where she almost always got her designer jeans and clothes, but God was calling her to a discount store. She felt that this store and others like it were for low-income families who couldn't afford better. The Holy Spirit was pulling her in the direction of that store, but her mind was already set to go to her normal place. As she got out the car, her mind and her legs were warring against each other. Her mind wanted one store, and her legs were walking toward the other.

She reluctantly gave in and decided to appease her spirit and take a quick look. She tried on clothes, which she hardly ever did, and after two hours, she purchased eight pairs of jeans, spending the same amount of money she would have spent for one designer pair. She praised God for allowing her to be delivered and set free from thinking she had to wear all the latest and most expensive fashions. Not only were the jeans much cheaper, but they fit better. If the truth was told, most brand-name jeans were designed to fit narrow frames, not people with robust, full-figured apple bottoms like Lynette's. She still shopped for quality—via designer or not—but she was no longer in a designer frenzy, and she would wait until the seasonal clearance to buy.

Emotional shopping was another reason Lynette found it hard to save and lacked in her finances. She shopped when she was happy and when she was sad. She shopped when she was going to a party or a banquet. She shopped to celebrate the sun going down and when there was a full moon. She shopped in the rain, on a plane, in a boat, or with a goat. She shopped here and there. She could shop anywhere. She was always trying to find a way to spend money.

One day the Lord spoke to Lynette and told her to go on a fast.

She thought, *Okay, Lord, that's easy. I can deny myself food for a couple of hours each day. Besides, I can stand to lose a couple of pounds anyway.* The Lord repeated His request, but this time she heard it more clearly: God wanted her to go on a *shopping* fast.

"Lord, is that You?" she asked. "Lord, are *You* talking to me?" She thought that somehow their wires had gotten crossed and she was hearing someone else's direction. "Lord, what are you trying to show me? What have I done that you are trying to ban me from the one thing that brings me so much pleasure? What lesson are you trying to teach me? Just tell me, and I promise I will listen."

God replied, "Good, then you will not have a problem with this request."

Lynette took inventory of what she had in her closet and felt that God's request was not so bad. She had so many clothes that she could stop shopping for an entire year and still not wear the same outfit twice. The holidays were over, and it was the last week in December. She imagined all the money she could save. *I can do it,* she thought.

One day Lynette was on the phone talking to a friend. Her husband was out of town, and she wanted to hang out. Lynette suggested that they meet at the mall, do a little shopping, and go out to dinner. And there she was, driving to a place out of habit, forgetting all about the shopping fast she was on. You see, shopping was like second nature to Lynette, so she was programmed to just do it.

On the way to meet her friend, an eighteen-wheeler collapsed right in front of her. It did not dawn on her that she was not following the will and plans God had for her. After much frustration, she decided to go home and call it a day.

About two weeks later, in January of 2005, she had just eaten dinner and decided to take a trip to the mall to walk it off. She was at the sales rack in one of her favorite stores, and there it was: the suit she had been eyeing for months. It was now on the seventy-percent-off sales rack. She was about to get the deal of a lifetime. As she reached for the suit, a loud blast echoed across the store. *That was such loud thunder*, she thought to herself.

As she proceeded to purchase her suit, she could hear yelling and screaming, followed by the footsteps of people running in her direction. Not knowing what was going on—or even caring—Lynette approached the cash register and was stunned to realize that she was the only person left in the store, and probably in the entire mall. She called out for the sales clerk because she wanted to get her suit. Her blessing was on the way! Right.

One of the workers noticed her standing in the middle of the store. She got Lynette's attention and motioned her toward the exit, where she and everyone else stood. Approaching the door, she could smell the fumes of what could have been gas. She dropped the suit and ran out of the store. As she walked sadly to her car, she could hear conversations about a possible attack or explosion. She could see and hear the sirens and lights of every available emergency vehicle in town, but she left the mall feeling bad because she didn't get her suit.

The gas fumes filled the air from blocks away. When Lynette finally made it home, the kids were watching the news, which had reported a gas pipe explosion outside the mall. According to the gas company, it appeared that a twenty-inch gas main buried six feet below the parking lot and connected to an eight-inch main, was the apparent source of the blast. The explosion had taken place between two establishments, one being the store where Lynette had been trying to purchase her suit. For months her nickname was Jonah, and we all know the Jonah story.

God has called all of us to a place of obedience, and just like Jonah, we try to hide and run away from what God wants from us. God had called Lynette to a shopping fast so she would save money. After her second attempt to disobey God, was she able to restrain herself and obey? You bet! Not only did she hold out for the next several months, but she was able to save thousands of dollars.

Finances are one of the main reasons for divorce. It is wise for a couple to discuss their financial obligations before marriage. In Lynette's first marriage, she informed her husband that she was not good with paying bills, so she left that responsibility to him. But he failed to tell her that he had that same problem. After phones and lights had been shut off, she realized that she needed to make some changes. She prayed and asked God for wisdom concerning this matter, and the Lord informed Lynette and instructed her on what to do.

Know what it means to establish and maintain a good credit record. Stop renting your furniture and appliances; you are paying triple the cost of buying these items from retail stores. Don't write checks when you know you don't have the money in the bank to cover your purchase. That's fraud. Don't use someone else's social security number (like your child's) to purchase items. Again, that's fraud. If you messed up your credit, don't go looking for a cosigner. It's not going to happen. Why should anyone trust you with his or her credit when you don't even care about your own?

When I think about the word *entrapment*, what normally comes to mind is a law enforcement officer who persuades a person to commit a crime that he or she had no intention of committing. So, when I think about the many ways that companies use advertisements, I realize that this is a form of entrapment. Because of commercials, sales papers, and coupons, Lynette and others like her are seduced to spend money they did not intend to spend. In the legal system, entrapment is considered a misdemeanor. If Lynette had tallied up all the ways she spent or lost money annually, the numbers would surely have been shocking.

By no means do I consider myself a financial planner, but I do know the tricks and plots that many people fall prey to—and the related costs and suffering. I also know that Satan is the culprit behind this kind of entrapment. He has committed a crime against each of us, and he needs to be put behind bars in the name of Jesus.

I pray that each of you will become free from your financial temptations so that you can help others, as I hoped I have helped you. If Lynette had known then what she knows now, she would not have suffered from the adversary's cunning sifting of her finances. I hope that others learn from the things Lynette suffered and do not fail prey or stay ignorant regarding their finances. If you pray and allow God to teach you how to become a better steward of your assets, He will show you other ways you can save and begin to live in abundance.

Note to teenage parents: Stop buying your babies all those fancy designer outfits. Children growing at a rapid pace, and before long, they will have outgrown them. People buy their children and grandchildren so many outfits that the clothes are given away before the children have had the chance to wear them twice. If your child is not in school, why spend so much money to make him or her look good for the babysitter? If your child is not doing well in school, invest in more educational things—unless you are preparing him or her to work as a department store mannequin.

For more information about the godly discipline of debt-free living, visit www.patriach.com/debtjt.html.

"The thief cometh not, but for to steal, and to kill, and to destroy: I am come that they might have life, and that they might have it more abundantly" (John 10:10).

CHAPTER 11

Spiritual Miscarriage: Born to Win

Above all, taking the shield of faith, wherewith ye shall
be able to quench" all the fiery darts of the wicked.
—Ephesians 6:16

As she sat in class trying to recall all that she had studied, Lynette struggled to complete the final exam to obtain her real estate certificate. The struggle was not because she did not know the material, at least not all of it. It was because of the annoying radio that echoed loudly throughout the classroom. It was football season, and the home team was playing in the championship game. Suddenly the professor screamed aloud with excitement as the team won the Super Bowl. The entire class went into an uproar of exhilaration, while the night skyline filled with the lights and sounds of fireworks for the victory.

Lynette sat in shock, as she had worked hard for months to get to this point. She was now entering her second phase of a long and trying process. Weeks had passed, and she had done nothing with the education and knowledge obtained from this real estate course. She thought about all the federal statutes and regulations she'd had to learn, including how to calculate a loan-to-value ratio (LTV/CLTV/TLTV) and all the other material. She felt that it had been a waste of her time, money, and energy. This class was supposed to prepare her to become a licensed realtor, but was she really ready to take the state exam? She wondered if she should study more or take more classes. Lynette struggled to remember why she had even bothered taking the class in the first place. She quickly gave up hope that this knowledge would develop into something profitable.

Lynette wanted to get a better job, but almost all of the decent and available positions required computer skills. She decided to make herself more marketable by attending another school to learn Microsoft applications. She wasn't the fastest typist in the class, but she was willing to invest the time, money, and energy to gain another skill. She quickly mastered all the training necessary to complete the course. Her thirst for knowledge in this field led her to experiment with the various programs to the point that she knew the ins and outs before they were taught to her. Excited about the new class, she went to school hours ahead of time, just to familiarize herself with the material.

Her determination to learn was known in the class and throughout the entire school. So whenever the system crashed, everyone assumed that she was the culprit. Through time and effort, her skills increased in Microsoft Word and Excel, to the point that she was offered a job working part-time for the school. It seemed that once she had achieved the much-needed knowledge, the computer field dried up, but she did not let that stop her. Instead, she found a job in accounts payable. As Lynette looked back over the long and hard months she had invested, she marveled over the knowledge and talent of her newfound skills.

Then there was her fascination with tax school, which gave her not only a new job but a new idea. She had heard that a person could make good money working part-time doing taxes. This kind of job was right up her alley, because it was seasonal, and she had a "seasonal" attitude about things. This meant that she was easily bored and would quickly look for something else of interest. This was an excellent way to make fast money legally, without the long-term commitment.

Lynette carried this unborn skill with the same fire, intensity, and zeal that she'd had with all the others. Her skill "pregnancy" was going as planned. She had met each requirement and had taken every precaution necessary. But because she was committed to doing the same things, she got the same results. Somehow Lynette never carried this birth to full term. Had she simply miscarried again, or had she terminated this "pregnancy" voluntarily?

All these events are referred to as "spiritual miscarriage," because God had impregnated Lynette multiple times with opportunities, and not once had she been able to carry them to full term. Miscarriages occur when there are abnormalities within the pregnancy that prevent a full-term delivery. The medical definition of miscarriage is "the spontaneous loss of a birth." Even though there are many disturbing aspects to a miscarriage—or missing out on an opportunity—Lynette was disturbed that no one had asked her *why* wasn't she able to carry theses "pregnancies" through "birth." No one had tried to launch an investigation as to why this abnormality had happened or what was wrong. Was there something that Lynette needed to help carry those births to full term?

Can you identify the cycle of failure in your own life? What has God impregnated you with that you could not carry through on? Is there an assigned midwife in your life to help you push past the pain and help you deliver what is in you? A midwife is a person who provides support and care to a person during labor and delivery.

There are three stages in the birthing process called *trimesters*. The first trimester is when a woman acknowledges the fact that she's pregnant. In this stage, seeking guidance and instruction is very important for the well-being of the developing "life." Instruction is needed to properly manage and maneuver toward delivery. As an embryo or idea develops, the wrong advice could cause complications or miscarriage. Miscarriage or abortion of this embryo kills the plans and destiny that this birth would have produced.

In the second trimester, the pregnant person has to come to the full knowledge that certain provisions for the birthing must take place. This is also the stage when a "fetus" or plan is in the working phase, and all the major structures are formed. Others become aware that this person is impregnated. Due dates, preparations, and celebration are also included in the process of this second stage. This person is able to feel the internal movement of the unborn and can begin to visualize and expect the delivery process to take place. Pre-labor pains may occur, because the pressure is at an all-time high and can become somewhat uncomfortable and scary. This second trimester does not eliminate the chances of miscarriage. Difficulties can take place, which can affect the plans for a happy and healthy outcome. If the person is not mature or strong enough to carry out the birth, this could cause problems as well.

The final stage of pregnancy is the third trimester, when the woman is preparing for the delivery. It is important to make a checklist to ensure that all the steps leading to a proper delivery are taking place. This stage also gives the person a chance to reflect on previous accomplishments. In this stage, the person is eager to deliver and to celebrate the birth.

This analogy describes the same steps used to prepare and develop a person's spiritual gifts. In Matthew 25, a parable tells of a master who gave his servants talents. Let's apply today's terminology to this parable.

God has impregnated each person with talents—like singing, playing basketball, or acting. He also has given spiritual gifts according to His will. People may have the gift of healing, the gift of giving, or the gift of prophecy. Talents are not meant to solely represent God. They are used to demonstrate what God expects of you. Are you diligent in carrying out your responsibilities fully with the gifts and talents God has given to you?

"Where there is no vision the people perish" (Proverbs 29:18). What are your purposes, your goals, and your plans? What are you working toward? How can you make a difference in your world of influence? Throughout life, Lynette had been faced with those same questions, both personally and professionally. She could not answer them, because she had no plan. "I don't know where I'll be next week," she would say, "and you expect me to see where I'm going to be in the next five years?"

One Sunday morning at church, the pastor preached a sermon called "Getting into a Rhythm." He talked about having a vision. *Not here, Lord,* she thought to herself. *Not at church too.* Lynette finally realized that she could no longer escape the questions she had been asked all her life.

She had questions for God regarding success and failure. She wanted to know how some people had fortune and fame and others didn't.

How did Chris Brown hit the top of the R & B charts at the age of sixteen? How did Michael Jordan know that his gift was in playing basketball—and then use it to lead the Chicago Bulls into six championships and to become MVP five times and be known as the best athlete in the world? What about Oprah Winfrey? How did she recognize her calling? How did she become known as the "queen" of talk show hosts in American TV? What about Beyonce? Who told her about her talent? How did she become a pop star veteran at the age of twenty-one, and how did she become the best R & B female performer? What about Fresh Prince? People didn't even need to use his real name to recognize him. How did his young man top the pop charts, TV charts, and the charts? What about Yolanda Adams and Condoleezza Rice?

"Lord," Lynette asked, "how do I bring to life the gifts and talents You've placed in me?" She cried out to God because she was tired of lack and financial struggle in her life.

"And it shall come to pass in the last days, saith God, I will pour out of my Spirit upon all flesh: and your sons and your daughters shall prophesy, and your young men shall see visions, and your old men shall dream dreams (Acts 2:17).

God told Lynette, *My child, read my word and study to show yourself approved.*

"What does this mean, Lord?" Lynette prayed. "I know I don't have to wait until my last days here on earth to enjoy the riches you have in store for me. I know my timing is not Your timing, but Your word says, 'Ask and it shall be given.' Now I am doing as Your Word has instructed me to do. I recognize that You pour out blessings upon us all, but can you please tell me how I can receive what you have for me? I tithe as You request, and I pray as You ask. And now that I seek, I want to be able to find. Lord, I'm knocking, and I need the doors of heaven to open up and pour me out such a blessing that I don't have room enough to receive it all—just like your Word says."

Lynette had questioned God to the point where she was exhausted. As she continued to read and search the Scriptures for herself, the word *vision* kept popping up. In fact, *vision* is mentioned over a hundred times in the Bible. She again questioned God about getting an understanding of what He was saying. God continued to reveal to her the connection between speaking, doing, and believing—and it finally hit her.

"And the LORD answered me, and said, write the vision, and make it plain upon tables, that he may run that readeth it. For the vision is yet for an appointed time, but at the end it shall speak, and not lie: though it tarry, wait for it; because it will surely come, it will not tarry" (Habakkuk 2:2–3).

The answer was to set goals and see visions. They had been a part of her life the whole time. If only she had known then what she knows now, she would have known that visions are like a blueprint or road map to destiny. We must talk about our visions with someone who will support our dreams and push us along the way. Visions can also be both spiritual and demonic, and an untrained ear will not be able to determine which voice to follow.

Lynette did not know that the voices that had led her to the present were not the voice of God. She'd had good ideas, but they were not God's ideas. She had been trying to do things she'd thought would give her success. She had been going by her own agenda, which did not allow her gifts and talents to work for her good. She had been doing things outside the will of God. Visions from God are supernatural signs that reveal revelation. God also warns us to "try the spirits" to see whether they are of Him. If you are a child of God, you should know his voice (John 10:4).

Visions give you a snapshot of your future. They help you set goals. They give you determination, motivation, application, boundaries, and lifestyle. Lynette had been stagnant all her life, stuck in a rut of darkness. The Devil did not want her to see the plans and destiny God had preordained for her, so she stayed in darkness without vision. Darkness is the opposite of vision, and as long as darkness exists, we are brainwashed by Satan into believing that things will not get better. Many are tricked into thinking that they do not deserve to prosper and that they will continue to live miserable and unfulfilling lives.

The Devil is the Father of Lies, and he has been lying to you. People have become comfortable with unproductive, unsatisfying lifestyles. Lynette had always had a desire to go back to school, but she lacked motivation. She took classes, attended seminars, and even received certificates of completion, but none of these added up to a degree. But there came a day, a moment when she realized that her determination had to be greater than her desire. She had to comprehend that, in order to get different results and move forward personally and professionally, she must set goals.

When you are in the process of setting goals, make sure they are specific and tailored to the gifts, talents, and calling that God has placed on your life. Once you put goals in place, they will inspire you to go the distance.

In the winter of 2004, Lynette returned to school to obtain a degree. It was a hard two years, but she was determined not to let anything or anyone get in the way of a dream she'd had for over twenty years. Besides, it was no harder than rising kids alone, which she had done. It was no harder than not having enough money to pay bills, which she had experienced. And it wasn't harder than living an unstable, unproductive life.

She studied like never before and even made the dean's list. If no one else was proud of her, she was proud of herself. She learned that having multiple "miscarriages" didn't mean that God would not impregnate her again. God had not given up on her, and He will not give up on you. He impregnated her with the writing of this book, and she carried it to full term. God knew she needed more education, resources, and abilities to be successful in writing this book, and the only way to get the job done was for her to return to school. God gave her another opportunity to carry out the plans and destiny that He had for her. We cannot afford to abort the mission God has given us. God has equipped all of us to do whatever He has called us to do. Thank you, God, for allowing Lynette to go back to school to gain the knowledge necessary to complete this book.

You see, Lynette's gifts and talents were part of God's calling for her to teach. Her first teaching job was at the youth center where she counseled people, but never in her wildest dreams did she think that she would write a book. Yes, she got the jobs she applied for. Yes, she was able to get anything she put her mind to. That wasn't the problem. The problem was that she had never put her mind to anything of value, worth, or importance. She had never thought "big" about herself. Lynette had never thought that she could do better than what she was doing. She had never wondered why, how, or the how much. She had never planned, and that was why she had never succeeded.

Lynette had never experienced thousands of dollars in her bank account until recently. She had never learned how to obtain a house or a new car. No one had ever told her that she could make it in spite of her past faults, mistakes, and sins. If she had known then what she know now, she would have understood that she couldn't tell her dreams to everyone, because some people are dream killers.

Dream killers will try to abort your destiny and hinder your process. They will show you a million reasons why your plans won't work and will discourage you from proceeding. The Bible tells us that Joseph told his brothers about his dream, and because of jealousy and ignorance, they tried to destroy him. Joseph had a lifetime of struggles because of dream killers, but God's fulfilled the expected end of Joseph's life.

Though some people turned their backs on Lynette, though the Devil sought to destroy her, though the men in her life tried to stop her, though she was told she would never amount to anything, though no one had ever told her that she could make it, and though no one had ever told her what her gifts, talents, and calling were, she was like Maya Angelou's poem: "Still I Rise."

"A man's belly shall be satisfied with the fruit of his mouth; and with the increase of his lips shall he be filled. Death and life are in the power of the tongue: and they that love it shall eat the fruit thereof" (Proverbs 18:20–21).

CHAPTER 12

Lottery Boy: Bloodsuckers

There hath no temptation taken you but such as is common
to man: but God is faithful, who will not suffer you to be
tempted above that ye are able; but will with the temptation
also make a way to escape, that ye may be able to bear it.
—1 Corinthians 10:13

Late one night, as she tossed and turned to get some much needed sleep, Lynette decided to watch a little TV. As she channel-surfed, she ran across something very disturbing: a reality TV segment that exposed extramarital affairs and cheating partners. According to the disclaimer, the episodes were actual stories of common people who had hired private investigators to document and film the infidelity of a spouse or lover.

Lynette was dismayed because the episode was about a thirty-eight-year-old woman who was dating an unemployed twenty-three-year-old boy. "What were you thinking?" Lynette yelled at the TV. Her first thought was: what would possess a working, well-to-do, older woman to date a man who was fifteen years younger and unemployed? Have we women gotten so desperate that we are falling for anything?

Anyway, the woman on the episode had hired a team of investigators to follow her man, and sure enough, he was cheating. The confrontation portion of the program allowed the clients to confront their mates. When the team was able to corner this young man, he was outside the apartment, moving their stuff while accompanied by his new, older girlfriend. Someone out there, please explain to me why a woman would take a much younger man into her heart, apartment, and finances and then be shocked that she was solely responsible for everything in the home. Did she seriously think that this bloodsucker was going to pull his own weight? Seriously? Lynette was perplexed by the fact that this young, unemployed boy had become such a player.

How could people be so blind and desperate that they could not see the leeches sifting them like wheat? A leech is a bloodsucking worm, and scientists say that their bites may not appear harmful, but *human* leeches will bleed a person to death. They will suck their way into a person's heart, emotions, home, and finances, leaving their victims limp and lifeless. The best protection against such a loser is to acknowledge his or her true worth at the start. Get to know that person's heart before you introduce him or her to your pocket.

Leeches are generally small, but they will gorge themselves during a feed and will rack up enough to sustain themselves until the next feed. Once a leech is done feeding off you, it will drop off, going about its merry way and on to the next prey. Leeches need to recognize that there is no future for them when they base their prosperity, accomplishments, and happiness off the sweat and labor of others.

When God gave Lynette this revelation, He showed her that there was no difference between leeches and playing the lottery. She was no expert on playing the lottery, but she researched enough to learn that there are many different ways to play and win lotto—from Scratch-offs to Mega Millions. Leeches use people in much the same way that people play the lottery. People choose from a variety of options when playing lotto, just as leeches randomly pick and play people until they hit the jackpot. Leeches are willing to invest a couple of dollars into relationships, with the hope of hitting the wallets and purses of their prey.

Your mate shows early signs of financial struggle, and being the loving partner that you are, you lend a helping hand. You put him through school and help him straighten out his credit by paying off his bills. You keep the IRS from garnishing his income tax refund, by assisting with child support or school loans. You keep him from being evicted by dishing out more cash toward his mortgage or rent. You even sponsor a car payment to keep creditors from repossessing his car. Silly you, all in love, eyes glowing and heart throbbing, thinking you're in a committed and solid relationship. Then one day you get a phone call, and it's your mate, telling you that this relationship is not working out and that he wants to start seeing other people. As you sit and try to figure out what went wrong, take out a pen and pad and tally up all the money you dished out to help this leech.

Leeches don't consider the time they spend with their victims a complete waste of time, because they have many good memories. Their only motive was to hit the finances and get in and out of their mates' pockets like a thief in the night. While their hosts were caught up in the frenzy of the relationship, they were strategizing the cost of their time and attendance based on their perception of the potential for financial funding.

"Take my yoke upon you, and learn of me; for I am gentle and lowly in heart: and ye shall find rest unto your souls" (Matthew 11:29).

God's desire is for us to prosper and to be in good health. The Word tells us that we are to be as wise as a serpent but as gentle as a dove (Matthews 10:6). We should watch out for wolves in sheep's clothing (Matthew 7:15), because people are deceitful. The Bible also tells us that we wrestle not against flesh and blood but against principalities, powers, rulers of darkness, and spiritual wickedness in high places (Ephesians 6:12). The Devil will find any nook or cranny that he and his imps can squeeze into and cause havoc. He will use anything or anyone to bleed us of our good health, peace of mind, and finances. As we study the Word of God, we also need to learn about the works of the Devil so that we can be equipped and fully furnished unto all good works (2 Timothy 3:17).

When the "lottery boy" is on the move, he prowls around like a roaring lion (1 Peter 5:8), seeking someone to devour. He looks to manipulate and feed off those who are easy prey. Lottery boy can also come in female form.

You become a target because of the leech's perception of you, and perception is everything. You walk around in your designer colognes and brand-name clothes. You are well-groomed and well-respected. You have a fancy car and a diamond ring. You are the envy of their eye. Instead of putting in the same hard work and sweat that you've put in, they latch onto you to get what you've got. Not everyone falls into this category, because there are those who seek a "trophy" spouse, knowing that the exchange is beauty for finance.

If we find true love, a person's financial status should not matter. The Bible instructs us to always pray (1 Thessalonians 5:16–18), but we also need to watch, listen, and search the heart and intent of the person we are with. The Bible warns us to know who labors among us (1 Thessalonians 5:12).

One of Lynette's male friends was in this type of relationship. Joe worked two part-time jobs at local retail stores. His lady friend Cheryl was an attorney with her own private practice. Joe's relationship with Cheryl inspired the title of this chapter: "Lottery Boy." Many like Joe search high and low to find a partner who will put them in a situation where they hit the jackpot. Joe had the financial benefits of being with someone of higher status. Joe had Cheryl so discombobulated that she couldn't see how he was draining her financially.

Women, are we at a point where we don't know our self-worth? What has happened to our self-esteem? How long can we indulge in charity cases? Do we enjoy being a crutch to a cripple, a wife without a husband, a mother to a mama's boy, or a shelter for the homeless? Are we supposed to do a credit check on a potential mate or future prospect? Is there some way to know that if we marry this man, he can support his family? Have women climbed the corporate ladder so high that we can't find a man who brings an equal amount to the table? Or are we altogether lacking in common sense?

These questions are not meant to bash, crash, or smash your game. This is a call to all women, as well as men, who need and deserve more. Make your requests known to God, and stop settling for second-rate relationships. Women, stop being so eager to do anything to prove to "your man" that you love him—especially through your finances, with little in return.

How many men do you know who are waiting for their girlfriends to get out of jail and marry them? How many men do you see dragging their babies to a correctional facility to visit the babies' mamas in jail? How many men do you know who are willing to put up with baby-daddy drama in order to be with a woman? How many men do you know who will date a woman without a job, who is living in her mama's basement and is on drugs? How many men do you know who would allow their lady to lay up (be unproductive), to eat all the food by her married self, and to promise to leave her husband—and still be married ten years later?

Do you know a man who stays with a woman who beats, robs, and rapes him, calls the police to have her arrested, goes to post her bail (with a black eye), and doesn't press charges? Do you know a man who lets his girlfriend use their house to sell drugs, who gets caught—and then does time for her? Do you know a man who has witnessed his lady in bed with his best friend or who has gotten an STD from her—even as she denies it, flipping the script and saying it's all *his* fault because he doesn't give her the attention she needs—and then he forgives her and all is well?

Now, take those same questions and name the women you know who would put up with those things, and you can see my point exactly!

Note: more women than men are arrested and do time in prison for drug trafficking—in the name of love and loyalty.

"Finally, my brethren, be strong in the Lord, and in the power of his might" (Ephesians 6:10). Ladies, keep your standards high, because the more you lower them, the more likely you will find yourself looking up from the bottom of a barrel. Stand up and stay strong. Stop apologizing for your success. Stop feeling guilty that you've made it in spite of the odds. Stop allowing people to talk down to you and convince you that you will never measure up—which is what you must want, I guess, if you stay glued to that leech.

"But ye are a chosen generation, a royal priesthood, a holy nation, a peculiar people; that ye should shew forth the praises of him who hath called you out of darkness into his marvelous light" (1 Peter 2:9). You belong to God, and because He has called you into a royal priesthood, you should not wallow with pigs. When you purchased your house, you got it appraised for its worth. You look at the "blue book" to see how much your car is worth. Some of you even have the nerve to see how much he paid for that ring. But when it comes to knowing your own worth, you are clueless. Know your worth!

Lynette's first mistake was feeling that she needed a man to define her. It wasn't until her separation from her husband that God revealed to her that no one could show their true worth the way Jesus did on the cross. When Jesus died on the cross, He showed us that we're worth dying for. Our lives are so precious to our Daddy God that it must grieve Him when we sell ourselves short. Even the leeches around us know our worth. That's why they latch on and suck as much blood as they can before we notice.

Lynette dated a brother who had the mentality of a leech and drug dealer. No, he was not selling drugs on the corner—or using them, for that matter—but this man had a guaranteed method to hook and crook any woman he wanted. This man was good-looking, well-groomed, and well-built. He had good conversation and was very intellectual. He was not afraid to cry and show his emotions, and he had many qualities that we all dream of. This man had only two things in mind: conquer and destroy—just like a drug dealer on the corner, selling his pharmaceuticals.

Now, here's the deal. Listen closely to this divine revelation. A drug dealer in a new neighborhood wants his users (prey) to think that his product (body) is the best on the market. He purposely gives more per ounce than any other dealer in the area, and it is the purest around. The first sample is free. The second sample is discounted. Once he has you sprung (wanting more), you seek no other. You will leave the house early in the morning or late at night to have more of it (him). You will forsake all others just to have another taste of his product (body). You will find yourself hooked on him and him alone, doing things you thought you were too old or educated to fall for. The only way Lynette was able to recognize this spirit was through prayer. This same man had no car, bad credit, lived paycheck to paycheck, and robbed Peter to pay Paul (took from one thing in order to pay for something else).

In the end, when we come out of this zone and look back at it all, we begin to see that this person's job has been to show us a good time. In return, we have paid for the time he has spent with us, and before long, we have spent thousands of dollars on a person who may not have been worth a dime. If we want to avoid this type of relationship, we must pray to our Daddy God. Keeping God in the center of everything we do will keep us from the hurt, heartache, and financial pain of leeches.

Offer your body, your mind, and your soul to God as a living sacrifice. Give Him authority to work on your behalf so that you can discern the spirit, heart, and intent of those around you. You may have family members, friends, or even coworkers who are always leeching. Learn to say no! God can and will show you the truth, if you ask Him which doors to close and which ones to open. God will kill the things that need to die in your life, and He will raise up the things that should have life. Humble yourself before the Lord, and He will lift you up.

"Now unto him that is able to keep you from falling, and to present you faultless before the presence of his glory with exceeding joy, to the only wise God our Saviour, be glory and majesty, dominion and power, both now and ever. Amen" (Jude 1:24–25).

CHAPTER 13

Unprotected: Family Feud

If the Son therefore shall make you free, ye shall be free indeed.
—John 8:36

One day while at work, Lynette found herself standing in the midst of a conversation with two of her coworkers. As they talked about their daughters-in-law, one stated, "My son no longer has time for me, because he's always doing something with his wife." She went on to say, "I will never like her, and I curse the day they got married." The other woman started up about her daughter-in-law, saying that she wanted the young lady to address her as "Mom." She also complained that her daughter-in-law never called or came over, and the only time she got to see the grandkids was on holidays or special occasions.

Lynette quickly thought about her relationship with her mother-in-law. She could still hear the echo of her monster-in-law's harsh words ringing in her ear: "If I'd had my way, you would never have married my son." Somehow, the mothers of these men felt that it was the young wife's job to create a nurturing and loving relationship. As Lynette began to minister to these two women, she asked, "What have you done to welcome these wives into the family? Are you being good mothers-in-law? How do you address your daughters-in-law?"

Now, you cannot put all the blame on the mothers. If their sons loved and respected their own wives, they would not allow their dear, sweet mothers to interfere or disrupt their homes. Unsure if her coworkers were Christians, Lynette quoted a scriptural principle that is found five times in the Bible: for the cause [marriage] a man should leave his father and mother and shall be joined unto his wife and they shall be one flesh (Genesis 2:24, Matthew 19:5, Mark 10:7, 1 Corinthians 6:16, Ephesians 5:31). One of the women, who apparently knew some of the Word, yelled, "I hate that Scripture and the person who wrote it."

"What about the relationship between Ruth and Naomi?" Lynette asked. "Their obvious love was initiated by the mother-in-law to the daughter-in-law. Naomi must have done something to cause this Moabite woman to leave her home, adopt Naomi's God, and follow her mother-in-law back to her hometown. Ruth loved Naomi the way a biological daughter would love her mother."

Without any more words, the three of them parted ways. As Lynette returned to her desk, she felt angry about her coworkers' mentality. *What nerve!* she thought to herself.

"For if any be a hearer of the word, and not a doer, he is like unto a man beholding his natural face in a glass: for he beholdeth himself, and goeth his way, and straightway forgetteth what manner of man he was. But whoso looketh into the perfect law of liberty, and continueth therein, he being not a forgetful hearer, but a doer of the work, this man shall be blessed in his deed" (James 1:23–25 KVJ).

Note to mother-in-laws: I challenge you to take a good look in the mirror and ask yourself, "What manner of person am I to my son- or daughter-in-law?"

This comparison to a glass refers to a mirror, because it gives a reflection of what's in front of it, thus creating light or illumination, which produces truth. It shows the condition of a person's heart. In other words, are you mirroring God? Do your actions, deeds, and behavior reflect those of Jesus? What is the point of looking in the mirror if you see some things that need to be adjusted but you choose to ignore the obvious? The mirror's reflection also represents hearing the gospel and following the instructions. Avoidance will not change who you are or how others see you. Here is your chance to recognize your faults and change your reflection in that mirror.

It was July of 2003 when Lynette separated from her husband. God told her to write her story, express her feelings, and get it all out. It wasn't until two years later that this story was birthed into a book about healing and the removal of past disappointments, heartaches, and pains. If the contents of this book can give hope to the hopeless and strength to the weak, if they can encourage someone, somewhere that she has the power to change her situation, then *to God be the glory.*

In July 1994 many good things were happening to Lynette. She had just started working a new job, had gotten rid of the crazy ex, had purchased a new car, and had found a new church home. She was finally headed in the right direction.

Larry was the first person she met in her new workplace, because he was the one who interviewed her for the new position. They worked side-by-side, and before long they developed a work relationship. They shared personal experiences and appeared to have much in common. Both were single parents, and both celebrated their birthdays in the same month. They were sympathetic and emphatic to each other's issues and concerns.

On Valentine's Day, a coworker was celebrating a birthday, and all were invited. Larry and Lynette met at the party. They talked and laughed. It was a great indirect date, Lynette thought to herself. All eyes were on them as they danced the night away. The time drew on, and Larry decided to call it a night. Instantly, a feeling of loneliness filled Lynette's stomach, for a perfect night was coming to an end.

She walked him to the door. Their eyes locked, their hands touched, and his lips trembled as he whispered those three words that every girl longs to hear. He whispered, "I love you." She thought, *What do I do? What do I say?* And she did what every polite person would do. "I love you too," she responded. Was that what she was really feeling? All she could remember was that the night ended in a long, passionate embrace.

They never made a verbal commitment, but they both assumed that a relationship had started and that they were now dating. Larry and Lynette spent so much time together that they could not wait until the next day to see each other again at work. They wanted to keep their relationship a secret, so no one knew they were a couple. The strange thing about the relationship was that they connected in a nonverbal manner. Without saying a word, they knew each other's thoughts, plans, and intentions. They knew how to act in a professional manner without letting others know they were dating.

As their relationship grew, they learned that they were not as similar as Lynette had thought. They both struggled with "-holics"; he was an alcoholic, and she was a shopaholic.

"Don't fill yourself up with wine. Getting drunk will lead to wild living. Instead, be filled with the Holy Spirit" (Ephesians 5:18).

Larry loved to drink, and they went to parties together. She didn't see a problem with his having an occasional drink, until one night when he came over, stinking of booze. Lynette did not believe that her man was an alcoholic, because the only time she saw him outside the office was on Saturday, which he claimed was the only time he drank. Surely he was not an alcoholic just because he drank every Friday, Saturday, and Sunday night, was he?

Being a single parent with no support from the kids' dad, Lynette had to get a part-time job. The pay was good, and things were looking up, but the more she made, the more she spent. The only free time she had for Larry or for socializing was on Saturday evenings. She came home from work, cooked, assisted with homework, put the kids to bed, and had maybe an hour for herself. At the end of a very long and tiring day, Lynette still had enough energy to call Larry and say, "I love you. I miss you, and I'll see you in the morning." If they hadn't worked together, they would not have seen much of each other. Surely a relationship wasn't wrong just because a man didn't offer to help his woman in need, was it?

Larry was promoted to supervisor, which made things a little different. The company for which they worked forbade relations between supervisors and employees. Lynette and Larry knew that their relationship must stay a secret, although a few people knew they were dating.

One morning, Larry called Lynette into his office. He wished her a happy birthday and handed her a small, square box. She returned to her desk, scared to open it. Surely a man wouldn't give a girl a ring unless he intended to marry her, would he? The gift sat on the desk for several hours. She finally mustered up the nerve to open the present, and yes, it was a ring.

Now, a proposal is one thing a person understands. Two people go to a romantic setting for soft music, candlelight, and good karma. The man gets down on one knee and asks the woman these words of sweet melody: "Will you marry me?" Sitting at her desk, she tried to comprehend what would possess him to give her something like this at work. Without a word, she placed the ring on her finger, and instantly people noticed. "Are you engaged?" they asked. Not knowing how to answer, she responded, "Well, today is my birthday, and it's just a friendship ring."

Three years later, Larry and Lynette got married.

Their blended family was challenging at first. They had to get the kids acclimated to sharing parents and living quarters. The kids turned out to really enjoy having each other around. Like many siblings, they had their share of fussing and fighting, but it was the adults who seemed to have the real problems. Dr. Jekyll (the good personality) was gone, and Lynette was introduced to Mr. Hyde (the evil, selfish personality). The in-laws turned out to be more like outlaws. Her monster-in-law made it clear that she did not like Lynette. This made life unbearable for her on many occasions, because they spent many holidays with Larry's family. Being the mature person God had groomed her to be, Lynette took the abuse for the sake of her family.

"Blessed are those who make peace. They will be called sons of God. Blessed are those who suffer for doing what is right. The kingdom of heaven belongs to them" (Matthew 5:9).

Lynette's family could not believe what was going on. They knew the old Lynette, and they were shocked that she was taking so much from this man, his mother, and Larry's entire family. Many of Lynette's family members wanted to seek vengeance on Larry's family for what they were doing, but Lynette defused the flames. She wanted to make her marriage work, because she had failed so many times in other relationships because she could not commit. She was determined to hold on and hold out, so she thought she was doing right by her husband, the kids, and mostly God.

Larry spent most of his time playing ball during the summer months, and hanging out and getting high the rest of the time. There were many occasions when Lynette went to watch him play, and she knew it was going to be an all-day event. Even as she showed her support, she found that she didn't fit in, because all the other wives were drunk, high, or both.

On one particular day, after cheering and sweating for hours, she decided to take her husband out for dinner. Waiting for him to acknowledge her presence, she finally left the park by herself. Going back home alone, she cried out to the Lord about how faithful she had been for six long years.

She reminded God that she had endured many years of this man's lying, cheating, drinking, and coming home all hours of the night.

"Lord," she cried out, "according to your Word, you said that You have come that I might have life and that more abundantly. What kind of marriage is this, when I don't have a husband? What example is this for my kids to see? Lord, I do not want my son thinking that this is how he is to treat his wife. I don't want my daughters thinking that it's okay for their husbands to disrespect them." She continued to cry out to the Lord on many nights, trying to find the answer to what many others like her go through.

Finally, her husband came home drunk again. As her blood boiled in anger, she decided to go downstairs to talk with him. Although he was passed out on the couch, she woke him up, because she needed to talk. He was not pleased with the questions and the anger in her voice. He rose up in rage, yelling and blaming Lynette for the problems in their marriage. He said, "It's not my fault that you don't have friends to hang out with."

She thought to herself, *What a joke.* She knew that the discussion was not going anywhere, so she proceeded to leave the room. He jumped up and charged her from behind. She was not sure if he was going to attack, so she quickly ran upstairs and locked the door behind her. He kicked the door in, and in fear, Lynette pressed the panic button on the house alarm.

Larry went to jail that night. She had not intended for this to happen, but this man—her husband, best friend, and lover—had mentally and verbally abused her for the last time. She couldn't sympathize over the two days he spent in jail, because she felt that her marriage was a life sentence without a chance for parole. She had spent the last two years locked up for a crime of passion they both had committed six years ago, but Lynette was the only one doing hard time.

Lynette stayed true to Larry. She denied her flesh and the advice of others and devoted her time and energy to making her marriage work. But every time she wondered if she was being unfair, she dropped more of her standards, until she found herself lying flat on the floor with footprints on her back. He walked over everything she thought a marriage was based on. Her world—all of her beliefs, hopes, dreams, emotions, strength, love, and life—was torn, shredded into tiny pieces of nothing.

Lynette was close to her grandmother. Until December 22, 2003, when she passed away, Lynette visited her every Saturday to take her grocery shopping, do laundry, give her a bath, and comb her hair. She thanked God for her praying grandmother, who had introduced Lynette to God when she was twelve years old. She didn't know where she would have been if it hadn't been for her grandmother's prayers. She knew that God had kept her when she was lost, even when she didn't want to be kept. The prayers of the righteous grandmothers avail much. Thank God for all praying grandmothers.

Note to grandmothers all over the world: Continue to pray and seek God's face on behalf of your families, because prayer changes things. Your words penetrate the heart of God, and He will come through for you.

"Don't team up with those who are unbelievers. How can righteousness be a partner with wickedness? How can light live with darkness? (2 Corinthians 6:14 NLT). Larry and Lynette were apparently unequal. She believed that this passage of Scripture was telling her that when you team up with someone whose values, morals, lifestyle, and beliefs are different from yours, the burden of the relationship will weigh more heavily on the neck of the believer, choking him or her to death. The one having the faster and more selfish pace will drag the other painfully by the neck. Not only is this painful, but it is unproductive.

Once Larry had uncovered who he really was, Lynette found that they had little to nothing in common. He was a night owl who loved to drink, party, and hang out. She had no interest in doing any of those things. Lynette thought that she would be better off if her marriage was over, but the truth of the matter was that she was not sure what she wanted. All she knew right then was that she was separated from her husband and felt totally alone.

"No, despite all these things, overwhelming victory is ours through Christ, who loved us" (Romans 8:37).

Most people in Lynette's situation would normally call a friend, but she did not do so. This thing she was going through was too big for friends to handle. What could they do? What could they say? Her friends were going through similar problems. How could they help her? Who could truly understand what she was going through? Why burden them with something that they might not be able to comprehend?

This time she spoke with God, and God alone. For the first time in her walk with the Lord, Lynette found herself hopelessly devoted to God. She spent the first two weeks isolated from everything and everyone—just her and God.

When you experience true intimacy with the Father, you come out stronger, wiser, and so much better. We want the blessing of the Lord, but we don't want to go through anything to get it. Lynette finally understood that the Lord would get the glory in her jacked-up situation. It wasn't easy, and it hurt. At times she found herself wanting to call her husband. Sometimes she called, and sometimes she didn't. The fact of the matter was that God was the only one who could deliver her. God was the only one who could comfort her and mend her broken heart. Prayer changes things. Cliché or not, it is the truth.

"Stand fast therefore in the liberty wherewith Christ hath made them free, and be not entangled again with the yoke of bondage" (Galatians 5:1).

As she looked back over the years, the tears, and the fears, Lynette knew that she was still there by the grace and mercy of God. We all have a purpose in life, and she believed that her trials and struggles were not only for her own sake but for others out there who were going through similar issues. She now hopes, in the name of Jesus, to help young girls, teenagers, and other women who want to break free from the bondage that has been plaguing women for decades.

Once the respect, care, and love has left a marriage, what more is there? Yes, Lynette wanted her marriage to work. After her relationship with Anthony, Larry was the second man Lynette had poured her all into. Time after time, she pleaded with her husband to seek help, to seek marriage counseling, but he wouldn't. She made a covenant before God that she would love, honor, and forsake all others because of this man she called her husband. He was the one and only person she wanted to spend the rest of her life with. Yes, he had problems. What men don't? No one is perfect. But the Father is holy, righteous, and without fault. They could have worked things out—if they had been working for a common goal.

In the midst of her divorce, Lynette felt that God had already released her from this man. No one can speak for others who are going through a rough patch in their marriages, and Lynette knew what the Bible said about divorce, but she felt she was freed without condemnation. If her husband did not want to spend time with her, it was his loss.

We need to learn to love ourselves in order for others to love us. We must learn how to spend quality time by ourselves, without feeling the need to have a man around. Enjoy the point of life you find yourself in right now, and in due season, God will bless you with your soulmate, if you desire Him to. Just pray.

I do not advocate divorce, and I would never tell anyone to walk away from his or her marriage. I can only share what happened with Lynette. God is the only one who will judge you, so make sure you are operating in His will. The way Lynette handled her situation may not be right for yours.

Here is a prayer you might say for your husband:

> Father, in the beginning I chose my past partners, but now I pray that You, Lord, will prepare me to be a wife and send my soulmate to me. With Your guidance and tutorship, I will learn the true meaning of love. Show me how to be submissive and what it truly means to be a virtuous woman. I now know that marriage is a covenant between three—a husband, a wife, and God. I promise that once I am joined to my soulmate, I will love him and only him.
>
> I promise to relinquish all duties that I now hold as head of house over to him. I will know my position in the home, which is to be a help to my husband, not a hindrance or burden. I will not feel inferior to my husband. I promise to be a wise woman who builds up and does not tear down, encouraging but not discouraging. I promise not to use my body as a tool but to recognize that my body belongs to him and him only. I thank You for blessing me with this man of God as my husband. For these and all other blessings, I thank You in the mighty name of Jesus, amen.

CHAPTER 14

Wireless Connection: No Dropped Calls

You will call out to me for help. And I will answer you.
You will cry out. And I will say, "Here I am."
—Isaiah 58:9a

In the marketing industry, companies like to use catchy phrases to draw our attention to their products via commercials. Every wireless phone company wants to be the leader in the global communication market. They come up with catchy phrases like:

- we never stop working for you
- support you can count on
- raising the bar
- bringing the family closer
- whenever, wherever

When I decided to get a cellphone, I did not know what plan to get or even what company to choose, because there were so many out there. They all had the same basic plans and promotional phones. What put one company above the rest? How could a person tell which company had the most reliable and affordable service? When I needed to get a call through, who could I turn to?

Having the right connection makes all the difference in the world. When I try to call family members who have a particular carrier, I usually get recordings that say, "The subscriber you are *trying* to reach is being located," "still trying," or "please enjoy the music while your party is being reached." As the carrier attempts to connect, I am forced to listen to loud, obnoxious music. And let's not even talk about the dropped calls. I can be in the heart of a conversation when, all of a sudden, my phone is silent.

I don't know about you, but when I have an emergency, I don't want to listen to music while my call is being placed. I don't want to get "your line is being checked for trouble" when I have a real and present situation. I don't need a voice mail recording telling me that someone will get back to me at their earliest convenience. How can these wireless companies promise that they "will never stop working for you," when I can't connect to the person I need when I really need them the most? How can a company simply say, "Whenever, wherever." What does that mean, when I pass a certain area and my phone call drops? Answer this for me: what sense does it make to start free minutes at nine p.m.? Whom does this benefit? And if other wireless connections offer the same guarantees, what makes any of them exclusive?

What if I told you that I know of a wireless connection that you can call "whenever, wherever"? What if I told you that this same connection will never stop working for you? It has no hidden fees, no monthly bills, no dropped calls, no overages, and no roaming. This connection is, in fact, the support you can count on. It is simply the easiest to use, and it is guaranteed to bring your family closer. If I could combine all the other wireless carriers' promises and put them together in one package, would you be willing to try this connection? You will never get a busy signal, because you will always get through. This surely raises the bar for all other services you will ever experience.

Are you willing to try a connection that will keep your hands free while driving—without those annoying headsets, car kits, cases, or clips? This connection does not run on a battery, so you will never have to worry about a low cell charge, nor will you ever need to upgrade. You will never again have to yell to the caller, "Hold on! I dropped the phone."

There truly is such a plan! The carrier is God, and the connection is prayer. It's a direct line to help. Prayer will get you answers to questions that others may not have the resources to give. The conversation you have in prayer is confidential and private, between you and God. It gives you instant relief from the anxiety of the day. It's comforting to know that the lines are never busy, down, or tied up. There is no static, interruption, or bad connections. There are no hidden fees, time limitations, restrictions, or overage. Prayer is available day and night, on weekends and holidays. Prayer is your best "whenever, wherever" wireless connection.

"Pray without ceasing" (1 Thessalonians 5:17). The Bible commands us to pray. When the disciples asked Jesus to teach them to pray, He gave them one of the best examples to follow. Jesus knew the importance of prayer, which was why He gave us a template to use while praying.

"After this manner therefore pray ye: Our Father which art in heaven, hallowed be thy name. Thy kingdom come, Thy will be done in earth, as it is in heaven. Give us this day our daily bread. And forgive us our debts, as we forgive our debtors. And lead us not into temptation, but deliver us from evil: for thine is the kingdom, and the power, and the glory, forever. Amen" (Matthew 6:9–13).

Lynette remembers one night when her crazy ex-boyfriend Walter called to say he was going to her harm her for all the stuff she had put him through. She knew his mind was twisted, and she'd had to get an order of protection to keep him away from her. When he called, she gave him a few choice words and hung up the phone. As she lay there, contemplating whether or not this joker was for real, the Holy Spirit instructed her to get

Wireless Connection: No Dropped Calls

up and go to the living room. She turned on the TV and fell asleep on the couch. She had forgotten that this man knew her every move, and he had remembered that Lynette kept a spare key to her apartment in her car.

She woke up just in time to move out of the way when he attempted to hit her in the head with a car jack. She sprang to her feet and ran into the kitchen. He came after her, grabbed two kitchen knives, and hemmed her in on both sides of her body. She could tell that this man was not himself. When he looked her in the eyes, it seemed that he was looking right through her.

Lynette began to plead with this demonic spirit that reminded her of all the bad talk she had heard earlier over the phone. The more she pleaded, the more he pierced her in her side. She had to stand on her toes because of the way he held the knives. She could tell that he was trying to puncture her lungs.

Who could she turn to? Who could she call? Lynette was not close enough to a phone to call the police. She could not call her girlfriend and say, "Girl, guess what," or call a neighbor for assistance. She needed help right then. It did not matter whether she had AT&T or Verizon, because their wireless connections required that she have the phone in her hand to dial for help. Even if Lynette had had voice command on her phone, she would have needed access to the phone to connect. Prayer was the only connection that could bring her out of that situation. Thank God for His wireless connection on that day, because if it wasn't for prayer, Lynette would not be here today to tell her story.

There was another incident when Lynette relied on her wireless connection and understood the importance of prayer. One night while coming home from work, she was approached by a young man. It appeared that he was trying to get into the building, and without thinking, Lynette allowed him access. He pulled a gun out of his coat pocket and pointed it at her, demanding money. What wireless connection do you think she used to

151

call for help? God is the only wireless connection what will measure up to all our expectations. Prayer is the key that will unlock help in a time of crisis. If she knew nothing else back then, she knew that help was just a prayer away.

"At all times, pray by the power of the Spirit. Pray all kinds of prayers. Be watchful, so that you can pray. Always keep on praying for all of God's people" (Ephesians 6:18).

Have you ever been around someone who loves to talk, someone who seems to know a little about a lot? This is a person you might turn to for information, because you feel he may have some knowledge about a particular subject. You can call on this person, day or night, and he can always come up with something intelligent to say. You have a good sense that this person has it going on. But what would happen if you had a very important decision to make and this buddy, whom you would customary consult, is not around? We put so much trust in people that we forget to trust God.

Prayer gives us twenty-four seven access to God, the problem solver. Unlike your friend, God surely knows everything about everything. God is the jack-of-all-trades and the Master of everything. He loves it when we cast our burdens and cares upon Him (Psalm 55:22). When Lynette was immature in the things of God, she wanted to know why should she pray. If God knew her heart and her thoughts, wasn't that good enough? She felt that she would get the answer to her questions by thinking good thoughts.

Like most people who do not have a prayer life, she thought that all of her solutions would come by attending Sunday school, Bible class, or a morning sermon. This didn't change until the day that God whispered gently in her ear and began to ministry to her. The only way the Father can have a good relationship with His children is if they spend time together. The only way a person can know the purpose and destiny for his or her life is to question God, the one who drafted the plans, through prayer.

The quality time we expect from our mates is the same expectation God has for us. We spend time getting to know our spouses and trying to master the responsibilities of our jobs. We spend time doing chores, shopping, studying for exams, and just hanging out with our friends, but somehow we forget to schedule time with God. How else can we go to God except through prayer?

"Come unto me, all ye that labour and are heavy laden, and I will give you rest" (Matthew 11:28).

Prayer is not a drive-through where you place an order at the first window and pick up your request at the next window. Prayer is not like your answering service or voice mail, repeating the same message over and over again. It is not a powerless, run-of-the-mill waste of time, nor is it a fast, instant, express, ten-items-or-less line. Prayer is a way of life. It's a way to commune with the Father. It's where you can unleash and unlock opportunities. It's a time to be blessed by your heavenly Father. It's where your strength comes from. Prayer changes people, situations, and things. Prayer is where you receive healing, instructions, and direction. Prayer will cleanse you of all your sins and lift all your heavy burdens.

If you need deliverance, try praying. If you need healing for your soul, pray about it. If you need to learn to forgive or you have bitterness in your heart, pray. If you need your love ones to be saved, pray for them. If you have a test and want a passing grade, pray (as well as study). If you cannot sleep at night, or if you have no money in your pocket, pray. Prayer gives you a plan. It keeps you out of trouble and gets you out of tough situations.

Prayer allows God the authority to work on your behalf. It is how He unlocks the positive things in your life. If you want to improve your relationship with God, pray more—and study the Bible as well. There are different types of prayer that you can use to get the desired results. You wouldn't go to a doctor of optometry it you had a toothache, would you? This also holds true with prayer. Know how to pray and learn what type of prayer will get you the right results. Below are examples of the types of prayers that can help us as we make prayer a lifestyle.

Thanksgiving and praise: "Make a joyful noise unto the LORD, all ye lands. Serve the LORD with gladness: come before his presence with singing. Know ye that the LORD he is God: it is he that hath made us, and not we ourselves; we are his people, and the sheep of his pasture. Enter into his gates with thanksgiving, and into his courts with praise: be thankful unto him, and bless his name. For the LORD is good; his mercy is everlasting; and his truth endureth to all generations" (Psalm 100:1-5).

Petition: "Therefore I say unto you, what things so ever ye desire, when ye pray, believe that ye receive them, and ye shall have them" (Mark 11:24).

Agreement: "Again I say unto you, that if two of you shall agree on earth as touching any thing that they shall ask, it shall be done for them of their Father which is in heaven" (Matthew 18:9).

Healing: "And when he had called unto him his twelve disciples, he gave them power against unclean spirits, to cast them out, and to heal all manner of sickness and all manner of disease" (Matthew 10:1).

Intercession: "I exhort therefore, that, first of all, supplications, prayers, intercessions, and giving of thanks, be made for all men" (1 Timothy 2:1).

Binding and loosing: "Verily I say unto you, whatsoever ye shall bind on earth shall be bound in heaven: and whatsoever ye shall loose on earth shall be loosed in heaven" (Matthew 18:18).

Supplication: "Be careful for nothing; but in every thing by prayer and supplication with thanksgiving let your requests be made known unto

God. [7]And the peace of God, which passeth all understanding, shall keep your hearts and minds through Christ Jesus" (Philippians 4:6).

Communion: "But one thing is needful: and Mary hath chosen that good part, which shall not be taken away from her" (Luke 10:42).

Dedication: "Then saith he unto them, my soul is exceeding sorrowful, even unto death: tarry ye here, and watch with me. And he went a little farther, and fell on his face, and prayed, saying, O my Father, if it be possible, let this cup pass from me: nevertheless not as I will, but as thou wilt" (Matthew 26:38–39).

Affirmation: "For verily I say unto you, That whosoever shall say unto this mountain, Be thou removed, and be thou cast into the sea; and shall not doubt in his heart, but shall believe that those things which he saith shall come to pass; he shall have whatsoever he saith" (Mark 11:23).

Repentance: "Have mercy upon me, O God, according to thy loving kindness: according unto the multitude of thy tender mercies blot out my transgressions. Wash me thoroughly from mine iniquity, and cleanse me from my sin. For I acknowledge my transgressions: and my sin is ever before me" (Psalm 51:1–3).

Prayer + Obedience = Results

CHAPTER 15

Reflections: The Way Life Used to Be

For the weapons of our warfare are not carnal, but mighty
through God to the pulling down of strong holds.
—2 Corinthians 10:4 KJV

One late night as Lynette slipped into a deep sleep, she dreamed that she was awakened by the Holy Spirit. "Get up, get dressed, and follow me," the voice commanded. As He gently held her hand, they entered into what appeared to be the center of the earth. This place was dark, scary, and smelly. As fear gripped Lynette, she clutched tightly to the Holy Spirit's hand. He reassured her that there was safety in His presence and no need to be afraid.

As she walked, she could hear many screams and cries coming from different directions. She saw people locked in chains, prisoners in their individual cells. As Lynette walked past the prisoners, many began to call out for help, and the Holy Spirit answered them, saying, "I am here with you, even in the midst of the fire."

Lynette looked around, and it became clear to her that she was in the pit of hell. With eyes wide open, she wondered, *Why am I here? I've made some major changes in my life. What lesson am I to learn from this place?* Normally when Lynette had such frightening dreams, she would force herself to wake up, but not this time. She wanted to know the outcome.

Being all-wise and all-knowing, God heard Lynette's thoughts, so He began to explain to her that these people had died in their sins, and this was their final destination. They ranged from preachers who had used the church for personal gain, to false prophets who had lied and used their talents as fortunetellers. There were witches, adulterers, murderers, drunkards, thieves, liars, and fornicators, and everyone that operated in lust, gluttony, greed, slothfulness, wrath, envy, and pride.

Swish! A sound from above Lynette's head rang out. The screams of each individual echoed off the walls, and the smell of burning flesh filled her nostrils. She realized that this place called hell was real. It was a place of torment and darkness, the eternal place for those who died in sin. Each person acted out the sins they had committed while on earth. Then everlasting fire would come and melt their skin down like wax. The unfortunate part about this process was that each person was able to feel the effects of the consuming fire, but it was not the death of them. This was to repeat itself all day, all night, every month, for this was the sinners' eternal home and destination.

As they approached the next cell, the Spirit, who had accompanied Lynette through this awful, forsaken place, left her alone. As fear and terror tried to grip her again, she could hear that small but gentle voice telling her, "You are not alone. I am here with you." She continued her journey and noticed demons and imps that were busy supplying fire and hot coal to each of the furnaces.

She came upon the cell of a pregnant woman. When curiosity got the best of her, she asked the young lady, "What landed you here?" The woman expressed her fascination with competition and described how she had used it to seduce married men. She told about the many houses and families that had been destroyed by her lust, greed, and jealousy. She explained that a single day had made the difference: while driving down a wet road, she had lost control of her car and had died in her sin.

As the woman's life flashed before Lynette's eyes, God allowed her to see all the women and children who had been hurt because of this woman's selfish, sinful nature. As the imps and demons passed by, carrying more coal and supplies to the furnaces, Lynette understood the reason she was seeing all this. She knew that there was still something in her own life that needed to be made right. She realized that if she didn't change her ways, she too would be spending eternity here.

In the early years of Lynette's life, she had struggled sexually, physically, emotionally, mentally, financially, and spiritually. She had lived in her own torment right there on earth. The root cause of all her problems was the sin in her life. It had started twenty-seven years earlier, when she decided to partake in that one act of sin. She had become a single parent and had contracted an STD, which had derailed and delayed her going to college, which had caused more trouble, hardship, and sin. She had lacked direction and motivation. She did not know, nor had she been told, that there were side effects from one act of sin.

If you commit one sin, it is connected to other sins, which allow other demonic spirits to attack you. Generations that come after you will be targeted and will suffer as well. Knowing to do right and choosing not to do it is a deliberate rejection of the truth of God's Word. This is the spirit of rebellion and a form of witchcraft.

As Lynette grew spiritually, she came across a book entitled *Strongman's His Name, What's His Game*, written by Drs. Jerry and Carol Robeson. This book takes a biblical approach to the names of the strongholds that you may be facing. Below are examples of the areas wherein the people of God struggle. This will give you an idea of what curses are linked to your sin.

Perverse Spirit (Isaiah 19:14)

Manifestations	
Broken spirit, wounded spirit	Proverbs 15:4
Evil actions	Proverbs 17:20;17:23
Abortion	Exodus 21:22–25; 20:13
Child abuse	
Prostitution	
Masturbation	
Atheism	Proverbs 14:2; Romans 1:30
Filthy mind	Proverbs 2:12; 23:33
Sexual perversions	Romans 1:17–32; 2 Timothy 3:2
Doctrinal error	Isaiah 19:14; Romans 1:22–23; 2 Timothy 3:7–8
Twisting of the Word	Acts 13:10; 2 Peter 2:14
Molestation, pedophilia	
Bestiality	Leviticus19:23–30
Adultery	Leviticus 19:20, 24–30
Incest	Leviticus 19:6–18, 24–30
Rape	
Pornography	
Chronic worry	Proverbs 19:3
Self-love	
Contention	Philippians 2:14–16; Titus 3:10–11
Foolishness	Proverbs 19:1
Lust, fantasy, filthy minds	
Homosexuality/lesbianism, effeminate spirit, sexual deviation, perversion	Leviticus 19:22, 24–30; Romans 1:27
Vain imagination	

Evil actions
Frigid spirit
Fornication

Lying Spirit (2 Chronicles 18:22; 1 Kings 22:22)

Manifestations	
Strong deception	2 Thessalonians 2:9–13
Flattery	Proverbs 20:19; 26:28; 29:5; Psalm 78:36, Psalm 12:2–3; Job 17:5
False prophecy	Jeremiah 23:16–17; 27:9–10; Matthew 7:1
Gossip	1 Timothy 6:20; 2 Timothy 2:16
False teachers	2 Peter 2
Lies, deceit, exaggeration	2 Chronicles 18:22; Proverbs 6:16–19; 24:28; 1 Timothy 4:2; Proverbs 26:28
Slander	Proverbs 10:18
Accusations	Revelation 12:10; Psalm 31:18
Religious bondage	Galatians 5:1
Superstitions	1 Timothy 4:7; Acts 25:19
Profanity, cursing	1 Timothy 4:7; 1 Timothy 6:20; 2 Timothy 2:16; Psalm 10:7; 59:12
Seeker of man's approval	
Guilt, shame, condemnation	Jude 1:4; Jeremiah 3:25; Philippians 3:18–29
Homosexuality, fornication, depraved desires, lust, sexual perversions, sodomy	Romans 1; Leviticus 18; 20:10–21; Revelation 21:8; Proverbs 6:25; Matthew 5:28; 1 Corinthians 10:6; James 1:14–15; 1 John 2:16

Hypocrisy	Proverbs 11:9
Self-deception	1 Corinthians 3:18; Jeremiah 37:9; 1 John 1:8
False burdens	
Covenant breaking	Leviticus 26:15

For more information about the strongholds that control your life, visit www.booksofthebible.com/p6018.html.

Although you may not have experienced all of the curses mentioned, committing one or two can open the door and leave your children and grandchildren exposed to these attacks. Sin does not start and stop with one man. It creates havoc through your ancestors, you, your seed, and your seed's seed. Sin also carries many forms of side effects, just as medication does.

Whenever you take medicine for one problem, there is a risk of more problems accruing. Sin has the same negative effects as medication. You will be exposed to darkness, sickness, disease, depression, brokenness, bondage, misery, and attacks on family, which are linked to generational curses and death. When your temptation is allowed to grow, it produces sin, and when sin is completed, it brings death (James 1:15).

Lynette's dream had the same plot as the Charles Dickens story, "A Christmas Carol," in which the character Ebenezer Scrooge repented and changed. In order to demonstrate Lynette's need for change, God had to show her where her life was headed if she did not make him Lord of all and totally submit her life to Him. When Lynette finally awakened from what had felt like reality, she was coughing and gagging from the stench of burning flesh. Believe it or not, hell is real. This is not a place where one can even imagine spending eternity. What will it take to convert you?

"The Son of man shall send forth his angels, and they shall gather out of his kingdom all things that offend, and them which do iniquity; and shall cast them into a furnace of fire: there shall be wailing and gnashing of teeth. Then shall the righteous shine forth as the sun in the kingdom of their Father. Who hath ears to hear, let him hear" (Matthew 13:41–43).

When people think about the places called heaven and hell, they already have a picture in their minds. These two places separate the good from the bad, the right from the wrong, and the wheat from the tares. Can you imagine living in a community where crime, poverty, sickness, and disease do not exist? When Lynette and her husband were ready to purchase a home, they first had to find a realtor. The realtor created a profile of their needs, and they set out to find the prefect house. Each listing spelled out the specs of each home, from the number of rooms to the exterior.

With this information, they were able to choose from a list of homes that they felt were best suited to their needs. In the spiritual realm, there are only two homes to choose from. Below are two descriptions of eternal homes. This permanent residence has nothing to do with your credit history, the amount of money you make, your occupation, or how long were have been at your current job. You do not need to provide references or sign a stack of papers, and there will be no closing costs or home inspections. You will not need a loan officer to explain the difference between conventional and FHA loans, or what a PMI, ARM, or LTV is. Your criteria will be based on your own prequalifications, not those of your household. It will be based upon how you lived on earth.

Remarks about Heaven

Spacious acreage lies behind gates of pearl and driveways and walkways paved with gold. Fresh, living waterfalls and fountains are in every room of every house, and all are laced with the finest of silver, gold, and remarkable gemstones. There are cathedral ceilings in all rooms, and frankincense and myrrh fill the atmosphere with their aromas. The sound of angelic and celestial voices ring in the air. Large bay windows are dressed in the finest tapestry of purple linen and silk, and each cabinet and countertop is made from the finest and best-cut diamonds. This gated community is built by the Master craftsman and is guarded by the heavenly hosts.

Heaven is the kingdom of God (Acts 14:22); the heavenly kingdom where Christ is King (Revelation 1:6); God's own possession (1 Peter 2:9); the heaven of heavens (Deuteronomy 10:14); paradise (Luke 23:42–43); and the place of the joy of your master (Matthew 25:23).

Remarks about Hell

Hell is accessed by a one-way entry and is located behind a barbed-wired fence. Driveways and walkways are paved with fire and brimstone. Rooms are small, smelly, and cave-like. The aroma of burning flesh fills the atmosphere, and the voices of tormented souls ring loudly in the air. Fountains flow with everlasting, molten lava laced with sin's indulgence and burning flesh.

The sound of terror and the gnashing of teeth rips the air (Matthew 25:30). Hell is a place of outer darkness (Matthew 22:13). It is a place of torment (Luke 16:23), sorrow (2 Samuel 22:6), and everlasting destruction (2 Thessalonians 1:9). It is a place where men are tormented with fire and brimstone (Revelation 21:8).

If Lynette had known God then like she knows Him now, she would have known that hurt, pain, disappointment, rejection, failure, defeat, lack, sickness, and death are the side effects of partaking of sin, which originated from the depths of hell. Below are just a few of the blessings and curses that we all face, according to our acts of obedience or disobedience.

Heaven	Hell
Blesses (Galatians 3:13–14)	Curses
Healing (Acts 10:38)	Sickness
Joy (Matthew 16:20)	Sorrow
Peace (Philippians 4:7)	Misery
Riches (1 Samuel 2:7–8)	Poverty
Deliverance (Psalm 32:7)	Bondage
Rest (Isaiah 28:12)	Weariness
Life (Matthew 16:28)	Death
Comfort (Matthew 5)	Mourning
Light (1 Peter 2:9)	Darkness

Life – God = Death

What on Earth Do You Want?

"Let no man say when he is tempted, I am tempted of God: for God cannot be tempted with evil, neither tempteth he any man: but every man is tempted, when he is drawn away of his own lust, and enticed" (James 1:13–14).

What habit or addiction controls your life? What person, place, or thing tests your faithfulness to God? The Bible teaches that your demons—whether they are sex, money, or drugs—will entice and control your thoughts and actions. We give the Devil too much credit. He does not make us do anything that is not already in us to do. We can overcome the sin that has us in bondage.

"There hath no temptation taken you but such as is common to man: but God is faithful, who will not suffer you to be tempted above that ye are able; but will with the temptation also make a way to escape, that ye may be able to bear it" (1 Corinthians 10:13).

Every temptation we face in life is shared by all of us! There is always somebody, somewhere who has had to face the same enticement you face—and has overcome it. The good news according to the law of God is that every temptation we face has an attached escape plan or a way out. Satan rears his ugly head and whispers, "Go ahead and do it. You won't get caught. You are justified in your revenge." But you have an opportunity *not* to act on the thoughts that Satan tempts you with. There is an exit sign telling you to resist the Devil, and he will flee.

"I press toward the mark for the prize of the high calling of God in Christ Jesus" (Philippians 3:14).

In sports like football and basketball, each team presses toward winning. In archery, the goal is to hit the bull's-eye, and it requires certain skills and techniques. Knowing how to shoot your arrow makes hitting the mark possible. Hitting the wrong mark can cause damage to yourself as well as others. In life, all of us have goals, and we make plans to achieve these goals.

Is heaven your goal? If so, what preparations have you made to make sure you meet your goal? You no longer have to be a slave to sin. Deliverance for you has already been established at the cross. Walk in victory, and change the way you think, act, and live. Jesus Christ died for Lynette, and she now lives in victory. Because Christ died for you too, victory belongs to you as well. I hope that Lynette's life has encouraged you to look at that man in the mirror and make a change.

Follow me down the Romans road to salvation.

"For all have sinned, and come short of the glory of God" (Romans 3:23).

"But God commendeth his love toward us, in that, while we were yet sinners, Christ died for us" (Romans 5:8).

"Knowing this, that our old man is crucified with him, that the body of sin might be destroyed, that henceforth we should not serve sin" (Romans 6:6).

"Now that we be dead with Christ, we believe that we shall also live with him" (Romans 6:8).

"For the wages of sin is death: but the gift of God is eternal life through Jesus Christ our Lord" (Romans 6:23).

"That if thou shalt confess with thy mouth the Lord Jesus, and shalt believe in thine heart that God hath raised him from the dead, thou shalt be saved. For with the heart man believeth unto righteousness; and with the mouth confession is made unto salvation" (Romans 10:9–10).

"For whosoever shall call upon the name of the Lord shall be saved" (Romans 10:13).

"And be not conformed to this world: but be ye transformed by the renewing of your mind, that ye may prove what is that good, and acceptable, and perfect will of God" (Romans 12:2).

"For of him, and through him, and to him, are all things: to whom be glory forever. Amen" (Romans 11:36).

Sources

Lull, Raymond. "Seven Gifts of the Holy Spirit." *lullianarts.net/7gifts.htm.* (Retrieved December 12, 2007.)

Smith, Kathy A. "Biblical Descriptions of Hell." Fill the Void Ministries, *www.fillthevoid.org/Christian/Hell/HellBiblicaldescription.html.* (Retrieved September 16, 2007.)

"Committee on the Operation of the Abortion Law." (Ottawa, 1977): 321.

Trichopoulos, D. et al. "Induced Abortion and Secondary Infertility." *British Journal OB/GYN,* vol. 83 (August 1976), 645–650.

"Dating Violence Common among Teens." *www.family.samhsa.gov/talk/datingviolence.aspx.* (Retrieved May 3, 2006.)

"Domestic Violence Against Women." *www.godlovesyouforever.org/stop_domestic_violence_against_women.htm.* (Retrieved May 2, 2006.)

"Godly Discipline of Debt-Free." *www.patriach.com/debtjt.html.* (Retrieved June 21, 2007.)

"Good Housing Friend & Family Order Woman Younger Man." *magazines.ivillage.com/goodhousekeeping/myhome/friends/articles/0,,287164_545668,00.html.* (Retrieved May 7, 2006.)

Grimes and Cates. "Abortion: Methods and Complications." *Human Reproduction,* 2nd ed., 796–813.

"HIV Among Pregnant Women, Infants, and Children." *www.cdc.gov/hiv/risk/gender/pregnantwomen/facts/index.html.* (Retrieved June 13, 2011.)

Indiana Prevention Resource Center, Trustees of Indiana University. *www.drugs.indiana.edu/resources/druginfo/index.html.* (Retrieved May 2, 2006.)

Laurier, Joanne. "International Committee of the Fourth International (ICIF)." (January 15, 2004.) For more information, visit the World Socialist website.

RAINN: Rape, Abuse, Incest National Network. *www.rainn.org/statistics/index.html.* (Retrieved April 1, 2006.)

"Soul Ties 3." *www.b4prayer.org/soul_ties_3.htm.* (Retrieved November 19, 2006.)

"Soul Ties 2." *www.b4prayer.org/index11.html.* (Retrieved November 19, 2006.)

Robeson, Dr. Jerry and Dr. Carol Robeson. *Strong Man's His Name. What's His Game?* 1985, p. 53. *www.gatewayrevival.org/Intercession_Pages/warfare/warriors_manual/16strongmen/perverse_spirit.htm.* (Retrieved February 8, 2007.)

"Teen Breaks." *www.teenbreaks.com.* (Retrieved June 2, 2007.)

Massip, Al. "The Chess Center." *www.chess-center.com/lessons/beyond13.htm.* (Retrieved September 20, 2006.)

"The Fatherless Generation." *http://thefatherlessgeneration.wordpress.com/statistics/.* (Retrieved June 2, 2012.)

"The Glory of Heaven" is a copyrighted work taken @The Narrow Way © 1993 by William C. Nichols. It may be downloaded for your own personal use at *members.aol.com/wnichint/heaven.html.*

"The National Center for Victims of Crime." *www.ncvc.org/law/Stalking/stalking_frames.htm.* (Retrieved May 2, 2006.)

"The Real Armor of God." *www.realarmorofgod.com/armor-of-god.html.* (Retrieved February 28, 2007.)

"When Mothers Abandon Their Children or Families." *The Washington Times* (May 7, 2013). *communities.washingtontimes.com/neighborhood/steps-authentic-happiness-positive-psychology/2013/may/7/when-mothers-abandon-their-children-or-families/#ixzz2W77Ju6bq.*

Bradshaw, John. *Healing the Shame that Binds You. www.soulselfhelp.on.ca/tshame.html.* (Retrieved February 26, 2007.)

"Types of Prayer: Information about Prayer and Praying." ARTA Software Group and David P. Geller. *pws.gamewood.net/~engineer/pray.htm.* (Retrieved December 12, 2006.)

Daniels, PhD, Kimberly, Jo Jones, PhD. and Joyce Abma, PhD. "Use of Emergency Contraception among Women Aged 15–44: United States,

2006–2010." *www.findarticles.com/p/articles/mi_m1272/is_n2638_v127/ai_20954306.* (Retrieved February, 2013.)

"US News Health." *health.usnews.com/health-news/news/articles/2012/09/24/prescription-drug-abuse-drops-among-us-young-adults.* (Retrieved September, 2013.)

Klinger, Ron. "What Can Be Done about Absentee Fathers?" *USA Today (Society for the Advancement of Education),* July 1998. *www.cdc.gov/nchs/data/databriefs/db112.pdf.* (Retrieved November 14, 2007